LOVE, LUST AND TRAUMA

GREEN BALLOON PUBLISHING

The Author

Professor Dr Franz Ruppert is Professor of Psychology at the University of Applied Sciences in Munich, Germany. He gained his PhD in Work and Organisational Psychology at the Technical University of Munich in 1985.

His publications in English include: *Trauma, Bonding & Family Constellations: Understanding and Healing Injuries of the Soul* (2008), *Splits in the Soul: Integrating Traumatic Experiences* (2011), *Symbiosis & Autonomy: Symbiotic Trauma and Love Beyond Entanglements* (2012), *Trauma, Fear and Love: How the Constellation of the Intention Supports Healthy Autonomy* (2014), *Early Trauma: Pregnancy, Birth and First Years of Life* (2016), *My Body My Trauma My I: Setting up Intentions, Exiting our Trauma Biography* (2018), *Who am I in a Traumatised and Traumatising Society* (2019), all published in English by Green Balloon Publishing, Steyning, UK.

Ruppert has spent the last 25 years studying the phenomenon of traumatisation and developing a theory and method of working with unconscious and very early trauma which he calls Identity Oriented Psychotrauma Therapy (IoPT).

He teaches his theories and his practical work in Germany and many other countries including Brazil, Austria, Norway, Singapore, Switzerland, Britain, Ireland, Italy, Russia, Netherlands, Poland, Portugal, Romania, Turkey and Spain. He has developed his own therapeutic approach called The Intention Method.

About this book

"Sexuality can be the highest, most life-affirming, creative force, or it can bring out the greatest destructive potential within a person." F. Ruppert.

In this book Professor Franz Ruppert explores the nature of sexuality as a form of reproduction, as an expression of love and a source of incomparable physical and emotional pleasure. It can also be the source of extreme devastation and destruction, a powerful weapon in the hands of traumatised people.

With this book Franz Ruppert completes what he has called The Trauma Biography, a biography of traumatisation that informs and influences the lives of many from the very earliest moments. The Trauma of Sexuality is a consequence of the Trauma of Identity and the Trauma of Love, detailed in his previous book, *Who am I in a Traumatised and Traumatising Society*. He shows how sexuality is easily distorted and becomes a trauma within the family, and within society. With case studies, examples and detailed explorations of what sexuality is in different ages and societies, and how it can exist within us in a healthy way, Ruppert takes us through this complex and central life issue.

As always, Ruppert writes in an immediate fashion, with care and detailed reference to many sources on the topic of what sexuality is, and what makes it an origin of trauma.

LOVE, LUST AND TRAUMA

The journey towards a healthy sexual identity

Franz Ruppert

Translated by Lucy Jameson and Simon Lys

Edited by Vivian Broughton

GREEN BALLOON PUBLISHING

First published in the United Kingdom in 2020
by Green Balloon Publishing

German edition first published under the title
Liebe, Lust und Trauma
by Kösel Verlag

© 2018 Kösel-Verlag, München

For the English language translation: © Franz Ruppert 2020

All rights reserved. No part of this publication may be reproduced or transmitted in any form or by any means, electronic or mechanical including photocopying, recording or any information storage or retrieval system, without prior permission in writing from the publishers.

All case studies in this book are based on real events. In order to protect the identity of those concerned, names and, where necessary, personal details have been altered.

Green Balloon Publishing, Steyning
www.greenballoonbooks.co.uk

ISBN 978-1-8381419-0-5

Book production by The Choir Press, Gloucester
Set in Times

A healthy psyche can differentiate between:

- *I, you and we*
- *Past, present and future*
- *Real love and love illusions*
- *Sensual lust and sexual craving*
- *Life, surviving and death.*

Contents

About this book	iii
Foreword	xi
Sexuality – A Natural Force	1
Sexuality and the Psyche	14
Sexuality and Love	22
Sexuality and Identity	34
Sexuality and Society	48
Sexual Psychotrauma	79
The Trauma of Identity	97
The Trauma of Love	106
The Trauma of Sexuality	115
Identity-Oriented Psychotrauma Therapy (IoPt)	161
My Personal Conclusion	196
Bibliography / Literature	197
Notes	206

Foreword

What is sexuality? When is it a positive, and when is it a negative force? What are the circumstances in which sexuality is pleasurable and satisfying for those involved and when it is not? Why has it become the main source of stress for many of us? Why is it sometimes addictive? Why can sexuality turn into an experience that destroys a person's entire life? Why do some people feel so uncomfortable in their body that they would prefer to be the opposite gender?

Sexuality has many biological, psychological, sociological and political dimensions. Sexuality is not only of significance to all of us as individuals, and to our intimate relationships; the forms of reproduction and the way the sexes relate to each other create the bedrock of all our social interactions. Sexuality ultimately determines world politics.

I wrote this book because sexual psychotrauma is a common theme in my psychotherapy practice. Many people are desperately searching for solutions to their experience of this highly taboo and shameful topic. Meanwhile I have the theoretical understanding that can explain the reasons for sexual trauma, and I have developed a practical method for therapy which can support people to look at this issue.

My appeal to the public is to take the phenomenon of sexual psychotrauma more seriously. In my opinion, it is not helpful to continue working with vague concepts such as 'abuse' or 'sexual violence'. If we do, we will just continue to stumble around blindly with a layman's understanding of what is happening, moralising excessively, and exhausting ourselves managing the increasing mountain of symptoms rather than seeing the true causes. If we continue like this, we do not do justice to the victims of psychotrauma, nor do we ever come to understand the perpetrators, in order to break the cycle of their endless and senseless actions.

We all have to understand the highly complex victim-perpetrator dynamics within our own psyche, otherwise we continue to be at the mercy of these dynamics. Only by understanding our own psyche can we break free from a society that continually traumatises us, and start to develop constructive ways of living together (Ruppert 2019). Our sexuality holds tremendous creative potential. When we begin to embody our sexuality in a way that is less burdened by psychotrauma, this potential can give us, and others, much mutual pleasure and delight.

I am not a father. By my early twenties I was fed up and tired of changing nappies, bottle-feeding, potty training and pushing prams around the little village where my family lived, because that's what I'd had to do for too many years in my childhood for my four siblings. As the eldest I had to support my overburdened mother, who had to go out to work due to lack of money in our family. Once I could go away from home I didn't want to give up my newly gained freedom for the sake of 'family and children'. For me, the life that I had experienced with my parents and relatives wasn't something I wanted to repeat.

In my late twenties, as I developed a growing intellectual and critical awareness, I did not want to bring children into a world that I had experienced as deeply threatening to me. By the time I had personally developed sufficiently to have reached more inner stability I was in my forties, and despite repeated IVF attempts, it was too late for me to become a father with my wife. Realising this was at that time a very painful process for me.

Meanwhile I understand that my fear of having my own children had its roots in my early childhood experiences: it was only by good luck that I survived my first year of life. My parents didn't want me, and I only survived the time in my mother's womb by splitting myself off from the traumatic experience of not feeling wanted and not loved. I almost died in a traumatic birth process, my infant cries were silenced with brutal violence by my parents and I almost starved to death because I was not breastfed long enough and weaned too early. As the tiny child of traumatised parents who, because of their own trauma, were unable to show loving feelings, my isolation and loneliness were so great that I almost resigned and gave up on life. In this environment – this is now clear for me – it was not possible to develop my own sexuality within the framework of a healthy identity.

Because I am a man, and therefore only truly know that one gender from the inside, I do not want to claim in this book that I have a neutral stance on sexuality that I could present here objectively. However I do consider myself a scientist, critical of ideologies and one who values facts more than mere opinion or doctrine. I hope that I am meanwhile shaped enough by a strong scientific attitude: I am happy to have my misconceptions challenged as I gain fresh insights, or when others convince me of something previously unknown to me that I was not yet ready to think about or understand.

Psychology is a subjective science created by psychologists and, of course like every subject, I have my own blind spots. As a practicing psychotherapist over many years, on the other hand I can look back on a considerable number of empirical case studies of people who have been sexually traumatised. However it is also clear to me that I cannot recognise my own personal blind spots when it comes to sexuality. In order to do that I need the reflection of my fellow human beings, critical debate, and to be accompanied myself by a competent psychotherapist. Once a month I do a piece of personal work to enable me to get closer to my own true identity, and embody my sexuality in a way that is constructive, both for myself and for others.

In this book when I use the male grammatical form it always refers to both men and women, unless expressly stated otherwise. This also includes those people who do not feel they belong to any one gender.

I am again full of gratitude to John Mitchell as the publisher and Vivian Broughton as the translation editor for enabling another book of mine to be available in English. Lucy Jameson and Simon Lys did excellent work to make the German *Liebe, Lust und Trauma* available to English speaking readers. My thanks also to the team at the Choir Press for their careful contribution. Thank you all deeply from my heart.

Munich, May 2020
Franz Ruppert

Sexuality – a natural force

One of life's highs or lows?

Sexuality can be the highest, most life-affirming, creative force, or it can bring out the greatest destructive potential within a person. Sexuality can lead us to the emotional highlights of our lives, and it can let us sink into the pits of despair. It can be the most wanted or the most feared thing in a man or a woman's life. It can inspire the imagination into something transcendent and it can render someone speechless. Human sexuality can be the epitome of good or evil.

What provokes this extreme range of sensations, feelings, ideas, thoughts and actions in regards to our sexuality? Is there a natural force at work, which we humans are completely at the mercy of, an elemental power that we will never be able to tame, whether by religion or morality, through constitutions, laws or with our intellectual capacities? Do we constantly have to sacrifice ourselves to the arousal of our instincts, the orgiastic discharges of our bodies, and the unconscious hormonal, micro-biological and macromolecular processes within us? Do we have to declare rape, the sexual traumatisation of children, prostitution and pornography as 'normal' so that we do not go mad?

How can someone know himself if he does not understand his own sexuality? When he is driven by forces beyond his control, and does things that harm himself and others? In my twenty years of psychotherapeutic practice, I have come to understand that sexuality shapes the human organism from the very beginning of its existence, and influences nearly all our human behaviours. I know now that we urgently need an array of favourable developmental conditions for our sexuality to be fully integrated into our developing identity, so that it does not become a separate entity, spinning into the void, fostering death instead of life. I have been confronted with countless examples of sexual trauma in my practice, and I have been told many things that I would rather not have even had to imagine. I've learned why someone becomes a sexual offender, and I've understood why victims of sexual trauma are often unable to break away from their perpetrators, sometimes even loving their perpetrators and deeply mourning them when they are gone.

Why does sexuality exist?

Everything that lives is born, grows, reproduces (or at least tries to) and then dies. Life is constantly spawning new life. In the most basic forms of life, a living being simply divides itself (for example an alga, a bacterium or a mould) resulting in new independent beings. Plants multiply through buds and seedlings. As each individual species pursues this purpose, the population continues to grow unless it becomes limited by external conditions (scarcity of food or energy, change of climate, predators). Asexual reproduction is simple and straightforward; it does not require a second living being to participate – it creates 'children' who genetically match their 'parents' (clones).

When we talk of sexuality though, we mean reproduction that involves two sexes and an exchange of genetic material between the parents that produces offspring that are similar but not identical to the parents. This creates individuality, which serves two main functions:

- Parasites that might attack and kill the organism are less able to destroy an entire population.
- The myriad variations between the individuals make it easier to adapt to changing environmental conditions and thereby increase the chances of the species' survival.

Living organisms which are quite simple and whose environment which changes only slightly can afford to reproduce by cloning. However more advanced forms of life, that have to adapt themselves to different ecosystems, multiply by sexual reproduction, despite the extra effort and the significant risks involved in this type of reproduction.

Sexuality – A Natural Force

The goal with sexual reproduction is to produce a new combination of genes and chromosomes that are the basic building blocks of the living organism, which also leads to a prohibition of sex between too close relatives. In the animal realm (for example with bonobo monkeys that mate randomly), some kind of immunological parameters seem to be established in order to prevent fertilisation by one's own father or brother. In human societies incest is deemed a taboo, and sexual intercourse between family members is something that is seen as morally wrong. In addition, based on genetic research, it is understood that a union between close relatives leads to a higher chance of physical defects or mental disabilities in the children, because a defective gene that may be present in one partner cannot be cancelled out by a healthy gene from the other partner, because the gene base is too similar.

If we look through the history of the evolution of life on earth it shows us that the basics of sexuality have emerged gradually. Sexuality has developed in different ways and in many intermediate forms, such as hermaphrodites or self-fertilisation (Wickler and Seibt, 1990). Some species of fish can even change their sex several times depending on their age or the ecological conditions under which they live.

In some animals, like sea turtles for example, the sex is determined by the temperature at which the eggs incubate. In humans, however, the question of whether a child is 'male' or 'female' is pre-determined by specific chromosomes. If the egg and sperm come together with one X chromosome each, the child becomes female. If an egg with an X chromosome encounters a sperm with a Y chromosome, it becomes male. Up to the sixth week after the fusion of egg and sperm, all newly-conceived children still carry the potential for both sexes. Only after the sixth week do the genes develop the child into male or female. An XY chromosome pair mean that testicles, and later a penis, will grow; an XX combination leads to the growth of ovaries and a clitoris. The SRY (Sex-determining Region Y) gene located on the Y chromosome determines the direction of this differentiation; if it is absent the gonads will develop into ovaries.[1]

It makes a big difference whether the fertilised eggs develop outside or inside the parent's body. Female fish lay their eggs in the water; the male fish then sprays his sperm onto them and the spawn is then left to its own fate. Sea turtles bury their fertilised eggs in the sand, leaving the sun and the tides to take care of the rest of the process. Here the key for successful reproduction lies in the sheer number of fertilised eggs produced, the hatched offspring are left entirely on their own and are easily prey to other creatures. The principle at work here is generate many, because only a few may survive.

Birds, on the other hand, also lay their eggs outside of the female body, but then have to incubate the eggs themselves. After that both parents care for the young once they have hatched, until the offspring is fully-fledged and leaves the nest. The effort needed for this type of parenting reduces the number of 'children' a parent couple can to handle. In this case quality comes before quantity.

Even with us humans a mother usually only gives birth to and raises a single child. Twins that are born alive are the exception. If there are two fertilized eggs, one is often eliminated by the maternal organism within the first few days or weeks of pregnancy. Again the direction is clear: quality over quantity. Measures to reduce infant mortality also contribute to this trend. If nearly every child survives, that limits the number of pregnancies and births each woman has.

Sexual dimorphism

Biologically speaking there are only two sexes. The sex that has the job of the production of 'eggs' is called 'female'; the other sex, whose task is the production of sperm, is termed 'male'. From her two ovaries, a woman makes approximately 400 to 500 ova available for fertilisation during her lifetime, an average of one a month. Men, on the other hand, produce millions of sperm in their testicles every day.

Because in humans the egg is fertilised inside the woman's body and then gestates in her uterus for between 37 and 42 weeks, this results in a very unbalanced division of labour between the sexes in terms of reproduction. This leads to different characteristics in the male and the female body:

- The female physique must take into account the needs of both pregnancy (including a very elastic abdominal wall, and expansive pelvic shape) and postpartum childcare (including milk-producing breasts).
- The male physique can be more rigid. Men can concentrate their energies into the growth of only their own bodies and muscles. On average therefore they are taller and physically stronger than women.
- Men are slower to reach sexual maturity than women are, which means, amongst other things, the later onset of their fertility. Women become fertile about 1½ years earlier than men do. Here nutrition also plays a decisive role: the better the diet, the sooner girls and boys become sexually mature.

The different functions of women for 'childcare' also calls for important psychological differences – women must be able to adjust emotionally to the child. They need to be able to empathise and feel love for their child so that this sensitive, vulnerable individual who is utterly dependent on his mother can develop healthily. Every human being is in effect born prematurely and so needs intensive body-to-body contact with his mother for at least a year after birth. In comparison calves and other mammals can stand up and walk immediately after birth.

On a very basic level men have fulfilled their biological role after the sexual act. They are, at least on a physical level, back in the situation where they can look around for a new sexual partner. Only when they make the conscious decision to take on seriously their role as a reliable partner and father do they get the opportunity for emotional development and personal growth through contact with their partner and child (Garstick, 2013).

A rapacious lust for sex

In species where reproduction takes place outside the body and where there is no requirement for the parents to care for their offspring, the life of the male and female of the species seems to be a manic pursuit of sexual intercourse as frequently as possible throughout their life span, in a fierce competition with other members of the species. Sometimes a creature's own life will be sacrificed in pursuit of a successful sexual act, for example in the case of the praying mantis, where the female eats the male after he has fertilised her eggs in order to get additional protein (Miersch, 2002, p. 114).

In the animal realm sexual acts can also be violent. For example, several male dolphins will hunt a female dolphin and inflict physical injury on her in order to achieve their goal of mating with her. High status male baboons will ride on the backs of lower ranking males and penetrate them anally. Males and females will often behave like hunter and hunted; females are sometimes rounded up by males as victory trophies and policed as a harem. This form of sexuality is more stressful than pleasurable for both sexes. Sexuality and aggression under such conditions are often not easy to distinguish from each other.

To pass on our genes?

I don't hold with the notion that creatures that reproduce sexually do so to pass on their genes, because neither plants nor animals have the slightest idea what genes are. The urge to mate is as overwhelming as it is only because of the irresistible chemical attractants (pheromones), the rewarding hormones (dopamine, oxytocin), the key sexual stimuli, the pleasurable arousal of the sex organs. All of that combine together to bring the entire organism into an ecstatic arousal state that can only be relieved by the sexual act. For the animal world we have such words as 'rutting', 'heat' and 'frenzy'. Ecstatic feelings and orgasm experiences are incentive enough to crave sexual union, whatever the cost. The sexual contact with another living being becomes a reward in itself. Offspring is an inevitable result of that. The only way to avoid this is to take precautions and devise a suitable form of contraception. On an unconscious molecular level this is possible, but only the more highly evolved creatures like us humans are consciously capable of planning contraception systematically.

In the animal world the desire to have sex and the act of reproduction itself, are two separate things; this is also true for humans. The presumption that evolutionary biologists make that sex is primarily for reproduction, ideally as often as possible, does not ring true for us women and men, although of course there is an instinctive desire to reproduce in male and female humans. The 'desire to have children' can become very urgent at certain periods of life. However in the reality of everyday life, women are usually trying to prevent pregnancy. Men also may have a fantasy of fathering many children, but in reality they are more often frightened of the psychological, moral and financial responsibilities being a father would bring. So it is also the exception rather than the rule for men to have sex in order to become a father and taking on the responsibility of the child that may result from sex. Added to that, many men are afraid that they will be left 'holding the baby', when it is not theirs, because their spouse may also have had sex with another man.

It is well known that a large number of children in a family correlates to a lower level of education in the parents, a strong tie to cultural or religious traditions, ignorance of birth control or lack of access to contraception. Completely insane notions such as 'having sex with a virgin can cure AIDS' take it all one step further, and place the child in a world where no one cares about them at all. In addition, even in the richer countries, highly traumatised women are more likely to get pregnant accidentally, and we see more teenage pregnancies and women diagnosed with a mental illness to have repeated unplanned pregnancies. It should also be noted that highly traumatised men are more likely to become fathers, because they are not conscious of their responsibility for the child. A student on one of my seminars reported of a highly traumatised man, who already had three children and was not much of a father to them. He had barely separated from his wife and immediately got together with a new partner, who was shortly after pregnant by him.

Sexuality and humanisation

It seems to me that what is essential to the transition from the plant and animal world to the human world, is that parents do not see their children as objects that are interchangeable and can be treated as 'appendages or belongings', but rather are seen as individuals and subjects of their own life. For example, when a new child is born after a previous child has died, the new child may be given the name of the dead child. The child is then objectified and identified with the dead child. Once children are seen as subjects, each with their own individual needs and abilities, this will act as a conscious barrier for the parents to 'having children' and 'bringing them up' in any great number. In my view therefore this 'humanisation' takes place step by step as we bring our own subjectivity into awareness, and build our own subjective 'I' and personal 'want'. Once someone becomes conscious of themselves and their own humanity, they are then able to also see and value other people as subjects rather than objects. If, however, a person refuses to become conscious, and does not take such an opportunity if it is offered, then he should not be surprised if other people also treat him like an object. When men and women see themselves as subjects they will no longer debase each other as sex objects. When parents experience themselves as subjects, encountering their own individuality and consciousness, then they can also appreciate their child's uniqueness, and cherish and support the development of the child's own identity (Hüther, 2018). In this way as humans we can make the transition from merely struggling for survival to the common formation of a good life for all women, men and children. This would also be a blessing for plants and animals since we humans would value their life with much more respect than we do now.

Sex and sexuality

Often sexuality is reduced to mean purely sexual activity or sexual intercourse. To me that's a far too narrow viewpoint. 'The sexual act' or 'having sex' is only one aspect of human sexuality. To be a sexual being is the basic principle of a person's entire life from the very beginning. Even in the womb the ovaries of the next generation of women are created, and even there the unborn male baby experiences the first arousal of his penis. Any process of maturation for the human organism has fertility as its goal. A girl should become a woman capable of conceiving, and a boy should become a man of generative ability.

To compare oneself with one's own gender ('How pretty or strong am I?') or to advertise oneself to the opposite sex ('What do you like about me?'), to contemplate and choose a possible sexual partner, these are all gender specific behaviours that shape the perceptions, feelings, imaginations and thoughts of men and women all day long.

Because, even with us humans fertilisable ova are scarce whereas sperm are abundant, there exists, as often in nature, the phenomenon of 'female choice', an idea already put forward by Charles Darwin. Women choose their sexual partner, and this induces men to display their power and virility through body size and muscle mass, and prove themselves superior through status fights with other men. They compete amongst themselves and are generally less choosy than women when it comes to the opportunity to engage in sexual intercourse.

The onset of sexual maturity (puberty) in the body is well known to adjust the psyche of the child, who up until this point is essentially more aligned with the parents (Kasten, 1999). By the massive production of sex hormones, the outside world for the pubescent human becomes increasingly sexualised. Almost everyone is now scanned as to whether they are eligible for sexual contact. While this is true for all men from this point on until old age – and particularly 18-30 year old men under the influence of testosterone can become completely obsessed with sex – for women sexual desire varies depending on their menstrual cycle and their fertile days, and their interest in sex tends to fade with age. As women pass through the menopause they realise that they can no longer hold onto a desire to conceive. Vaginal dryness, which also increases with age, can make them shy away from sexual intercourse because it can be very painful (Tietz, 2017). Men, even in old age, can still entertain the idea of becoming a father, and since women often find older men attractive because of their higher social status, and men tend to prefer more youthful-looking women, becoming a father is still possible.

However, not just women's biological clocks are ticking. Male fertility decreases significantly from the age of 35 and the quality of their sperm decreases too as they get older. The chance of faulty mutation increases, and so the children may be more likely to have some kind of genetic disease. Similarly, the weight of environmental toxins in a person's body increases and this also can affect the health of the egg and sperm cells. So it is also the case that artificial insemination may become increasingly unlikely to fulfil the wish for a child the older the men and women involved are.

Masturbation

Already in infants it can be observed that they stimulate themselves through rhythmic pressing/rubbing and rocking movements (Bischof 2014). Sexual self-gratification (onanism, masturbation), the autonomous discovery of one's own ability to give oneself pleasure, until recently has had a bad reputation. Religious moralists have condemned it as 'the sin of self-abuse' (Metz 2017, p. 224 ff.), and even non-religious people talked about the detrimental effect on growth and vision, and warned amongst other things of how it can shrink your spine. The disgust against masturbating children has led to the introduction of male genital cutting, outside of the reason of religious rites, in America in the 19th century. "A remedy (for masturbation) which is almost always successful in small boys is circumcision. [...] The operation should be performed without administering an anaesthetic, as the brief pain attending the operation will have a salutary effect upon the mind, especially if it be connected with the idea of punishment." (Kellogg, 1888). Harvey Kellogg also had the brutal idea of applying pure carbolic acid to a girl's clitoris in order to break the habit of self-stimulation.

Even in so-called enlightened societies, masturbation is not much talked about. It is tolerated, but concerns about 'too much of a good thing' are often heard. But masturbation and the self-given pleasure of your own sexual experience is at least considerably better than:

- begging for sex
- getting sex only when there are certain preliminary performances like presents and gifts
- acting out our sexuality against the will of another adult
- going to see a prostitute
- sexually molesting children

For Hans-Joachim Maaz (2017), the art of pleasurably satisfying oneself is a prerequisite for exploring the entire terrain of pleasure together with a partner. However, as Heike Melzer (2018) observes in her sexual-therapeutic practice, some people can apparently no longer engage in sex with a partner, because they have found such sophisticated ways of self-stimulation that no one else can offer them. Masturbation seems to have increased these days, spurred on by constantly available pornographic material on the internet, and ingeniously designed sex toys, dildos, vibrators, and suction devices in such proliferation and intensity that many wonder why they need a sexual partner at all when they are able to have much better orgasms without one. It is not just men, but women too seem to take increasing pleasure from the small machines that provide them with hyper-orgasms at the touch of a button. The business of mechanically generated pleasure is booming worldwide; the machines increasingly resemble humans, and those who use them, in their trauma survival strategies, become more and more similar to the sex toys they use.

Penetration and lust

In humans, as in other mammals, the sexual act is remarkable in its particularity. A part of the man's body, the penis, penetrates the female vagina and intrudes deeply into the body of the woman. That is a massive crossing of a boundary. Because of this, many women are afraid of male sexuality, and many men are afraid that women will reject them. The sexual act demands the consent of the woman so that she does not experience this intrusion into her body as an act of violence. Similarly anal penetration, oral sex or 'French kissing' are massive violations of the physical boundaries of the female body. It therefore explicitly requires the 'yes' of the woman, so that acts like this are not perceived by her as rape.

When another person is physically too close to us this usually produces a stress response and a release of adrenaline. Aggressive defence or protection seeking behaviour accompanies this. Under normal circumstances, everything in a person will resist letting another person penetrate them, be it orally, genitally or anally, therefore it makes sense that the wish of women is that sexual intercourse is an exceptional situation that they themselves want and can experience as act of togetherness and love.

All the better then if not only the man, but also the woman, experiences pleasure and delight during the sexual act and reaches orgasm. Often sexual contact only becomes deeply physically satisfying for both partners through foreplay because the skin-to-skin contact, softly caressing, looking into each other's eyes and sensitive fondling all produce hormones (particularly oxytocin), which generate a feeling of wellbeing, security and freedom from stress and fear.

When I feel my own sexual desire, I can awaken the sexual desire in my partner, and that in turn further stimulates my desire. So together we both go on a journey to sensually charge each other's bodies more and more until we both explode into orgasm with each other's excitement, which then dissolves leaving both partners in a state of pleasant relaxation.

Fertilisation and becoming a mother or father

If the sexual act does lead to fertilisation, this does not mean sexuality ceases for those involved. Men will still want sexual intercourse. For women, on the other hand, this desire may lessen, because in her organism a reorganisation is taking place in preparation for the possibility of motherhood. However, it probably also depends on the state of her psyche, how healthy or traumatised she is, as to whether, or even how often, she will want to continue to have sexual intercourse.

Pregnancy, childbirth, breastfeeding and enjoying skin-to-skin contact with her baby are profoundly sexual events for the female body. If the man too is physically present and psychologically involved in fatherhood then it can also be a process for him that permanently changes and shapes his sexual identity.

Motherhood means becoming a mother; fatherhood means becoming a father – physically, psychologically and socially.

Sexuality and the Psyche

Typically male / typically female?

The more complex the 'hardware' of a living being is, the more sophisticated the software must become in order to enable the existence of the organism. Sexuality moulds the human psyche and the psyche steers our sexuality. Along with the instinctual and compulsive aspects of sexuality in humans come new experiences such as feelings, imagination and thinking. Sexuality in both sexes is connected with the whole spectrum of human emotions: from anticipation to joy, pleasure, lust, curiosity and pride to fear, anger, fury, disgust and hurt. We can go on sexual adventures in our fantasies and dreams; we can bring ourselves to sexual arousal purely with our imagination; we can plan systematically our sexual activities; we can evaluate what sexual contact is good for us and what is not; we can control our will in order to say 'yes' or 'no' to our sexual impulses.

Men are from Mars, Women are from Venus is a well-known book title. Popular tropes in books and films are, for example, 'why can't men listen?', and 'women can't park a car properly' (Pease and Pease, 2010). Men are portrayed as primarily rational and fixated on action and outcomes, whereas women are seen as emotional, needy and oriented towards relationship. Men are supposedly the stronger sex and women the weaker.[2] There have been numerous attempts to identify such differences between the sexes and attribute them to quasi-natural roles within social interaction. "Men always want to look at a woman's naked body, women always want to look into a man's naked soul". (Schwanitz 2001, p. 112)

Every human being is an individual and so unique in his body, his psyche and his actions. There are real differences between a woman and a man in terms of their physiology and psyche, because they have to fulfil different duties for the reproduction of the species. But whether these differences become opposites depends on the way in which women and men see themselves, how they grow together in communities, and how they learn to perceive the other gender. Those who are only aware of the world of gender from their own limited perspective may see women as incomplete men, or men as immature women. People who experienced early traumatisation and were forced to take refuge in survival strategies create many illusions about the opposite sex. He or she might easily feel threatened by it, sending them into an attitude of either submission or dominance. Moreover when society as a whole is based on competition rather than co-operation,[3] intimacy, love, partnership, parenthood and professional relationships will quickly become battlegrounds of men and women waging war against each other. It then no longer matters who the woman or the man really is, all that matters is how he or she appears to the others. From an early age, male children hear the message: Boys do not cry! And girls are told to be kind and pretty so they will end up with a good husband. Here is a small example of how gender stereotypes have continued to have a personal effect on me.

Does a 'man' do that?

Being born in 1957 I grew up with the typical gender stereotypes of that time. Men went out to work and earned the money, while women did the housework and looked after the children. The mess that my father made in the house from his building and carpentry work would have to be cleared up by my mother and us children. Since my mother also went out to work, we children had to take on many duties in the household. So, as the first born, I got used to cleaning, cooking and doing the laundry as well as feeding, washing and caring for my little brother and my three sisters. In this way at least I was able to get some form of praise from my mother. For everything that we children did my mother would always be ready with the warning 'What would the neighbours say?' This idea actually crept up on me many years

> *later when in my forties I was in the garden of my house in Munich hanging out the laundry 'What would people say if they could see me? Does a 'man' really do something like this?' The imprints of our childhood continue to work on us until we become aware of them.*

The definitions of what is male and what is female always exist in relation to each other. What is considered masculine or feminine in one particular era or generation is relative, and subject to historical trends. The middle-class ideal of the 'housewife' is a result of the male notion of a devoted wife who sees her own role as taking care of her husband and their children. This only works as long as enough women agree with this viewpoint and expect to benefit with a good life because of it. If women expect a 'real man' to be someone of a high social status with power and money, then men who want women as sexual partners will strive to be successful, whatever the cost is. If, however, the majority of women in a society would rather have men who are sensitive, who take their role as a father seriously and who behave with a sense of social responsibility, then men would have to orientate themselves to this and rethink their competitive behaviour.

The idea of a natural order of gender has nothing to do with actual nature, because we can see in nature how unfixed and varied the biological processes are when it comes to sexuality. For example, the male stickling after fertilisation takes on the task of guarding the spawn and caring for the brood, while the female moves on to look for a new sexual partner. In the realm of animals there is an almost infinite variety of reproductive strategies and tactics that males and females show. Even homosexuality and masturbation can appear in many different forms. If we look at the natural evolution of species, we humans seem to be closely related to chimpanzees and the bonobo monkey (De Waal, 2019). The males of the former are often very aggressive and compete with each other for the females, engaging the whole group in their rivalries. Bonobo monkeys, however, prefer to settle any conflicts that arise within the group with sexual activities – in accordance with the maxim 'make love not war'. They mate as the fancy takes them. Sex is not something in short supply, nor is it something that is only the right of the strongest and fittest (Miersch, 2002). Bonobos sometimes are so obsessed with sex, that some males will stick their penis in any available opening, even into a piece of metal tube.

The human brain, as the chief physical organ of our psyche, is also an argument against the idea of a 'natural' fixed set of specific behaviours for male and female, because the brain is extremely malleable, and changes its structure depending on how it is used (Hüther, 2009). This specifically makes the forming of 'I' and 'want' functions possible, which together can, if necessary, modify our instinctive animal impulses, preventing them from running wild (Bauer, 2015).

So the idea of 'nature' is only a thought construct, an idea of the human mind. 'Nature' does not really exist at all; it is not a subject that has its own goals and intentions. The idea of a gender hierarchy ordained by nature that forever defines the roles of men and women is an ideological construct that may be asserted by some men or women, or certain societies, states or regimes, for the specific purpose of serving their own interests, and thus forcing these roles to be generally accepted and not open to question. Those who want to maintain the supposed superiority of their own sex based, for example, on the word of a god or prophet, will only lead a life based on fear and aggression. Sooner or later all such rigid structures will become brittle and collapse, as a reflection on human history makes readily apparent.

So, for humanity it comes down to the basic question: Does sexuality embody the spirit of cooperation between men and women, or does it result in acts of violence? Do the genders love and respect each other or do they harbour rivalry and hatred? We humans can make the conscious decision to live out our sexuality in constructive rather than destructive relationships. And there is another good message for our present times: we do not have to manage our sexual impulses and desires alone; we can take the decision to seek psychotherapeutic help. We can all work together to stop the competition between nations or economies, and also end the battle between the sexes.

Sexual role models

Separation from mother and father

The development of human sexuality is not only a process of physical and psychological maturation; the young also need orientation as to what is sexually appropriate and what is not, within the social context in which he or she is growing up. Naturally children find their primary role models in their parents, girls in their mother and boys in their father, if he is available. If they are lucky, they will find something good to copy in their parents. But they may also be unlucky and have parents who are sexually totally confused. For example, I had no good role models during my childhood and adolescence in my parents or my relatives.

Where do my loyalties lie?

In my childhood I always sided with my stressed mother against my demanding father. This caused an internal split in me. My survival-self was bound to my mother, and my will to survive rebelled against my father. These were not good conditions for the development of my own healthy sexual identity. I was too busy with, and for too long engaged with my mother's problems and the conflicts between my parents. I struggled with the fact that there was always a new child arriving in our stressed and poor family, and as the first-born, I had to take care of them.

For boys, drawing a boundary between their own sexuality and the sexuality of their mother is more complicated than it is for girls. From the beginning the boy child is enveloped in female sexuality; in the womb, during the birth process, at breastfeeding, being held and carried, these all involve intimate physical contact with someone who is both their mother and a woman. This intense closeness can become sexualised for the mother; the sex and body of her son may arouse her. For the boy, this can easily slip into a sexual relationship too, if he is excited by the femaleness of his mother's body, and then as a man, he remains also sexually attracted to her. And, if the mother no longer has a sexual partner, the son perceives his mother's sexual neediness and may respond to it.

Under normal circumstances, the mother remains unattainable for the son. However, this may just increase his sexual arousal, and as an adult, shape his behaviour towards women in general. To ensure his masculinity a son must have the opportunity to distance himself from his mother, escaping her motherly and female temptations. This can be a hard inner struggle that takes a lot of energy. Perhaps this is why men search for masculinity as something distinct from femininity, as something clearly differentiated from their mother. So they may, for example, pat each other on the shoulder whilst giving each other a 'manly' hug, in order not to be reminded of the tender embrace of a woman.

For the daughter the separation from her father can be a difficult process too, particularly if her closeness to her father is eroticised or sexualised by him, perhaps because the older she gets the more attractive she appears to him compared to his ageing wife. The tendency on the part of the daughter to hold onto the 'strong' father is all the greater, the 'weaker' and needier she experiences her mother. Suddenly the daughter can harbour the fantasy that she is actually the better woman for their father. For such 'daddy's girls' later relationships with other men are also complicated, because the father is a third person in the mix. The age-appropriate separation from her mother is never going to be possible for a daddy's girl.

The internal struggle to disidentify with our mother and father can strengthen the healthy development of identity, helping to establish our own 'I' and our own 'want'. It all fails, however, when both the parents and children are traumatised, because the 'I' and the 'want' functions of the child have already been lost from early on. Because of this, such parents and children cannot experience true closeness, nor can they make a separation. Instead they cling symbiotically to each other, and at the same time aggressively push each other away. They are constantly switching between perpetrator and victim attitudes, and their sexual identity remains undeveloped.

Peers and the Internet

By the time we reach puberty, our peers have become our reference point for questions about sexuality and identity. What is currently the 'in thing'? Is it dressing seductively, smoking cannabis, drinking alcohol, playing sport, having a girlfriend or boyfriend as soon as we can, having oral sex ...? The range of depictions and advice that the Internet offers to satisfy a young person's curiosity regarding sexuality is nearly endless. It can lead to profound misunderstandings for the inquisitive adolescent, who may draw conclusions, for example, from pornographic videos as to how men and women should behave sexually: men as a constantly virile performer, and women as the ever-ready playmate for male enjoyment. In social and public media the mushrooming of dating sites offer the developing adolescent questionable models of sexuality, partnership and love. Even in a society that sees itself as sexually enlightened, good sexual counselling is still needed. Today's generation of adolescents need more competent points of contact in order to bypass the flood of sex, pornography, and dating services that the Internet spews into their mobile phones (von Weiler, 2014).

The development of a healthy sexuality needs a social environment that is sympathetic, supportive and able to explain the real facts of life. Children and adolescents need guidance from adults who do not condemn their burgeoning sexuality, but at the same time do not keep silent when stupid and wrong ideas form in the children's minds. In particular adolescents need to be educated against the idea that another person can be their property and used as a sexual object, because sexuality can be used to physically and psychologically destroy someone – both the perpetrator and the victim. Above all, adolescents need to learn to reconcile their exploding physical desires with their often still poor relational skills.

Sexuality and Love

The origin of love

In my training courses, when I ask participants "what does sexuality mean for you?" women in particular often say that they cannot imagine sex without love, and that they have always tried to see sexual intercourse as an act of love. In many languages we have the expression 'to make love' as a term for sexual intercourse.

Although it is sometimes claimed that love grows out of falling in love and sexual desire, there is far more evidence that it has its original source in the mother-child relationship (Precht, 2009, p. 162 ff.). The loving care that a mother can give her child, and the unconditional readiness of that child to love his or her mother, seem to be the primary source of all our loving emotions and behaviours. From the perspective of the child, in the beginning his love is instinctual; it is a basic need like eating or drinking, and this primal instinct is directed towards the mother.

If this loving connection between child and mother is not possible, then the child's need to bond will look for possible substitutes for a love connection. Bonding with someone who gives physical contact provides the child with what he needs and the protection against danger is imperative for the child. Therefore, even before birth, a co-developing twin can attract this love. In the absence of a loving bond with the mother, a father, a grandmother, a sister or a teacher can become a screen upon which the child's desire to be loved is projected; the less the child's own mother responds to his expressions of love the more intense becomes the desire for a substitute mother. Even when there is no one there, the child's psyche will invent in his fantasies substitute objects or substitute parents for his love. Some children who do not feel loved by their parents even think that they have been adopted, because surely their real parents would love them. Particularly heart breaking is the following example of a little girl who believed that she would have been better off as a baby animal than as a human child.

I am a lioness

In a research paper, a student of mine described a four-year-old child who claimed that she was not a human, but a baby lion. Sometimes she would walk on all fours, transform herself into a lion and crawl under the table. "I want to go back to the grassland. I want to go where the trees are green and the sky is blue. You know that I'm a lion. I miss my mummy and daddy so much. My real parents are lions like me. But they died in the jungle. So my human parents adopted me."

Strangers from birth on had cared for this child – a nanny would usually drop her off and pick her up from kindergarten.

It is a peculiarity of the human mother-child relationship that strong lifelong emotional bonds are built up; this is something that does not occur so markedly in the sphere of animals. Whilst it is true that animal parents can be highly committed, and consumed with care for the brood, providing their offspring with food and protecting them from enemies, once the period of brood-care is over, the children become rivals with their parents for food sources and territories. The proximity of the grown up children is an impediment to the parents' subsequent ability to produce more offspring. In the case of the cuckoo bird, who foists her egg onto another bird to hatch and raise, it becomes clear that brood-care behaviour is driven by instinct (triggers such as wide-open beak or begging shrieks) and not by loving emotion towards the offspring, since the 'foster' parent bird feeds the cuckoo chick as if it were her own. Something akin to a longer emotional bond only arises in mammals when the mother-child relationship lasts for a longer period, and if the young females remain part of the group, as is for example the case with elephants.

The loving emotions that develop in the bonding between mother and child, by the mother being present for the child, showing an interest in him, consoling and cheering him up, taking time for him, holding him in her arms and caressing him, all bear fruit for the child later when he grows up and comes into a friendship or partnership with another adult. The child who has experienced and learnt what healthy love is, who felt seen and loved by his mother and father can pass on this matured form of love into his later relationships. Gradually, as his own capacity for love grows, so does his ability to be in a loving relationship.

Therefore if those involved in a partnership have never experienced real loving affection and care as individual subjects from their parents as children, the love they experience together can only be raw and instinctual rather than real adult love. In this situation the partners will ask too much of each other in continual attempts to finally experience the love and emotional closeness that they did not receive from their parents as a child. "My husband or wife doesn't see me" is a complaint very often heard in therapy.

Children who receive too little love, or no love at all, remain instinctively attached to their parents, and continue to hope for love from them, even when adults and after their parents have died. This entangled attachment to the parents can become a major obstacle to the development of love in an adult partnership. In the worst-case scenario, one's own parents still exist in the psyche as internal psychological representations, even in the partnership bed. The partner is confused with a parent; he or she is idealised and also criticised, and has little chance of clearing up this confusion.

In general we should work on the assumption that our love/sexual partners are not just adults, but often have multiple split-off traumatised child parts in their psyche, that can easily be triggered within the relationship. Therefore, we can often find ourselves confronted with childlike behaviour in our partners that seem to arise out of nowhere, when they unintentionally transfer their unresolved feelings towards their mother or father onto us. The here and now then is overshadowed by the there and then. When these dynamics are blindly acted out and not well understood, the risk of a breakdown of the partnership is very high. Before I became aware of these dynamics of transference, I used to experience this struggle with my wife quite often.

Just like my mother!

> *I feel quite shameful today when I think back to how many times in the early years of our relationship I would say to my wife, "You're just like my mother!" Of course, there was, on her side, always the counter claim: "You're just like my father!"*

At the beginning of a person's psychological development, love, like sexuality, is compulsive and instinctive. Love and sexuality are located differently within the hormonal and neural networks of the body. Therefore, this begs the question as to how these two become interchanged with each other. Love and sexuality may or may not be connected with each other during a person's development. Instinctive sexuality can exist without love. Sexual stimulation, arousal and release can happen without any feelings of love. Sexual arousal can even happen when fear, aggression or pain is present. The biological aspects of sexuality still function even if the participants are severely traumatised and completely split off from their feelings.

This is demonstrated most in the fact that children can even be conceived when a woman is raped. Many women currently have to experience this painful truth while fleeing from terror and war in their home country, falling into the hands of gangs of men, who rape them, and then they end up becoming pregnant. Who can possibly expect such mothers to build up a loving bond with a child that was conceived through violence? Although on a biological level these women have become mothers, they are not mothers on a psychological or social level.

Artificial insemination, in vitro fertilisation, egg- or sperm-donation – all prove that children can be created technologically without any love. How these children feel is rarely the focus of those who cold-bloodedly buy and sell them.

If, through early loving support infused with feelings and

understanding by parents and other benevolent people, the instinctual love of the child can mature into a healthy partnership love, this also supports sexuality to mature in a healthy way. Only when sexuality is integrated into the overall personality, can interpersonal relationships be enriched and life become more enjoyable. The different psychological and physical potentials within love and sexuality combine in this way for a good life for those involved.

Falling in love, sexuality and partnership

People in a state of high sexual arousal are less choosy about a potential sexual partner than someone who is looking for the right person with whom to spend their future, have sex and bring children into the world. 'Partnership' is something other than a one-night stand. It is long lasting and goes beyond sexual contact. Common interests, hobbies or projects can give a solid groundwork for sexual passion.

There is much speculation as to what makes one person attractive to another: physique, face, hands, unconsciously perceived scents and odours, age, social status, skin colour – many things act as the decisive triggers when one person falls in love with another person, and wants to have sex with them.

Being in love is apparently a specific psychological state, into which a person can periodically fall through a certain cocktail of hormones (Precht 2009, p. 175 ff.). The target of one's desires then appears through 'rose tinted spectacles', where we only perceive their merits and hardly any of their faults. Our psychological world sometimes completely narrows down to this one person, whose closeness we seek and from whom we are hoping for a positive response in the matter of love. We also want to appear in the best possible light ourselves, and will do our best to cover up our shortcomings, and try not to make any of our weaknesses obvious. Hormones, like adrenalin, dopamine and serotonin, produce a state of over-excitement, giving us butterflies in the stomach, heart palpitations, making us feel weak at the knees and causing us to blush easily; they can also cause sleeplessness, and despair if our beloved one does not arrive on time, does not answer the phone or vanishes for several days from our landscape.

If the desire to be in love is reciprocated by the partner, then both can float on cloud nine for a while, spending sleepless nights with lots of sex, forgetting the world around and indulging in the illusion of a love that will last forever. But sooner or later this special psychological state of being in love disappears – it can last for a maximum of one or two years but sometimes only for a few days or even hours. Then the psyche switches back to its normal state, and the lovers are brought back from their dreams into the dryness of everyday life. The hormonal alignment of the psyche (men produce *less* testosterone in the infatuation phase, while women produce more) disappears and makes those affected less tolerant of each other's peculiarities. What was previously 'sweet' or 'cute' in the other suddenly becomes annoying and stupid. What becomes a habit gradually loses its appeal.[4]

Whether the lovers stay together as a couple, or they are hoping for another state of falling in love and go looking for the next prince charming or ultimate superwoman, is different from case to case. Those who stay together for the long haul at least can nourish themselves on sweet memories of their beautiful time of falling in love, and by this may survive many everyday arguments. Our partnership can become an opportunity to develop personally if, in moments of conflict, we ask ourselves: "What does this have in common with my biography? What am I repeating in the present moment that I have already experienced in my childhood? Which of my psychotraumas is currently being re-enacted between me and my partner?" In this way, a lasting partnership can become the engine for personal growth. Those who are quick to break up will definitely find themselves faced with the same unresolved problems in their next relationship.

Partnerships can provide a safe framework for each individual to develop personally, or they can become a lifelong prison. Which of these becomes the case depends, in my experience, on whether the partners have been traumatised as children, and are therefore unconsciously compelled to re-enact the pattern of their trauma survival strategies within their current relationships. The love that, as a child, we didn't get from our mother and father we can never receive from a partner as an adult. Partnerships can only be formed constructively if they are not weighed down by the traumatising experiences from each person's childhood. Hans-Joachim Maaz has developed a very comprehensive concept for a 'new culture of relationships' that should prove rewarding for every couple (Maaz, 2018). His book is worth reading.

Sexuality and parenting

The biological reason for the state of falling in love is the procreation of offspring. Falling in love reinforces the desire to have children and makes us willing to be monogamous for a while and build a lasting partnership. For this reason, falling in love is a good foundation from which partners can become parents. Pregnancy for a woman who is in love is the logical step when having sex, unless she takes precautions to prevent it.

It appears that women's wish to have children is generally stronger than that of men. Women change as a result of motherhood both physically and psychologically. In many societies motherhood also gives a woman a higher social status – in some societies to be a woman without children is to have no social standing at all. This alone is an important motive for many to become a mother. It also can be that men want to be fathers, not primarily because of their children, but in order to achieve the social status of 'father', and start a 'family', which is what their own parents, society or religion expects from them. This is also the reason why some couples expend enormous energy in order to have children, even resorting to costly or illegal methods, just so they too can say: "We are a family and therefore are normal."

However children can put a huge strain on partnerships. A pregnant woman's sexual appetite often recedes, and after birth she must practically and emotionally dedicate herself more to her child than to her husband. She will not wish to become pregnant again as long as she has a small child to take care of. Pregnancy, birth and childcare are exhausting processes. They deplete the body of a woman, remould her and often make her less sexually attractive to her husband. Previously fostered illusions of happiness and family can become increasingly fragile.

Here is an example from a member of my monthly men's group, whose self-encounter process brought him back to reality with a bump. Further explanations of the Intention Method as the therapeutic tool of Identity-oriented Psychotrauma Therapy (IoPT) and the resonance technique can be found in the final chapter of this book. In this book the Intention will always be written within double quotation marks, and the different 'elements' that are being resonated with will appear in single quotes.

My path?

A recently married man who had just become a father to a daughter came up with the following intention: "I am on my happy path". His resonance process however showed him the opposite. He was disoriented, without any connection to himself and in fact on a path getting further and further away from himself. His 'I' turned out to be a survival strategy, intellectualising and focusing on his partner and his daughter, and not in a position to effectively deal with his own intra-psychic processes. As the background of the Intention-holder's childhood history emerged, it showed he was all on his own while his parents fought with each other tooth and nail. He struggled on, on his own, being well-behaved and satisfying what was required of him. He is still loyal to his neglectful mother to this day. The child part of him, which was articulated by the person resonating with the word 'on' was therefore furious with him and felt betrayed by him even now. It was only when he was able, to some extent, to allow his pain to show up, which he had split off in his childhood, that a coming together of his split-off structures could take place. His survival strategy 'I' slowly stopped all his rational talking, sat down on the floor and left the path clear for something new to happen.

Men who hope to have guaranteed sexual satisfaction through marriage with a stable partner are often soon disappointed. Through having a child they lose their special emotional and physical standing with their wife. Many react to this with anger and frustration, withdrawing into their work or hobbies, or secretly looking for potential alternative sexual partners. For men, it is often hard to accept that their wife now relegates them to second place behind their child. In addition, the child is primarily emotionally bonded to his mother and in the early years perceives his father only through the filter of his relationship with his mother. Only when the child is older can he and his father succeed in establishing a direct relationship with one another, which is not coloured by the relationship with the mother.

The idea that a second child can revive a struggling partnership, back to its old freshness is a widespread illusion. Without identifying the reasons why we are together with our partner, and without working on the childhood conflicts that we have brought with us and which affect our partnership, a second child will only lead to being even more entangled in irresolvable conflicts, and ultimately to breaking up the partnership relation. Mothers then often find themselves single parents with two young children, exposed to the risk of poverty and hardship. Fathers may embark on a second marriage and start a second family, the longevity of which is similarly far from guaranteed. Many children then have to deal with parents who are living separately, still struggling to keep their unresolved relationship issues separate from their parenting as best they can, and manage the chaos of a patchwork family of multiple partners and offspring (Koschorke, 2013).

If sexually frustrated couples do stay together the children are at an increased risk of becoming substitute partners or secret (or overt) objects of their parents' sexual desires. Mothers may seek too much closeness with their sons, and fathers may inappropriately court their daughters.

When the sex life dwindles in a long-term partnership, there is also a risk that one of the partners, often the man, will start leading a double life. A man may then say, for example, to his partner that he has an important business meeting, when in reality he is going to a prostitute. Or he may browse pornographic internet sites to satisfy himself when his partner is away, until he loses the desire he originally had for his partner. Or he may secretly have a mistress, deceiving and lying to his partner to such an extent that it is clear that if his cover is blown the partnership is over, and his wife's efforts not to realise what is going on can no longer be maintained.

Family and work

Even if couples decide to stay together and to be there as equal parents for their children, this ideal quickly reaches its limits within a competitive economy. Women often only have the choice between three, stressful, options:

- Taking care of the upbringing of the children full-time and, therefore, being financially dependent on the salary of their husband.
- Working part-time and, with a guilty conscience, giving their children over to crèches, nurseries and day-care centres.
- Working full-time, with an even greater guilty conscience, as they fail to carry out their maternal duties and organise external childcare as much as possible (e.g. giving the children to grandparents for a few years) whilst still having to do the full-time job of looking after the household.

In a society geared towards economic competition and making money which chiefly increases the wealth of the wealthy, the work of reproduction counts for nothing compared to paid work. This leads to absurd situations such as a child educator dropping her own child at a kindergarten, before going to look after other children in another nursery.

Even if fathers are prepared to take more care of the children and be involved in domestic life, they are usually forced by competition in the professional world to keep on working full-time. Being a 'stay at home dad' is not well respected in most societies. In the industrialised nations, due to the small nuclear family model and the pressure towards job mobility, traditional family-based networks of support such as grandparents or aunts and uncles are generally no longer available nowadays.

It is possible that under this kind of stress fathers who decide to stay at home with their child, while the mother returns to work, are unconsciously living out their own unfulfilled childhood needs and their yearning to be mothered. This is also not a good situation for the child who needs a clear adult person as a mirror for his healthy identity development.

In capitalist societies the ideology is propagated that education is the foundation for personal success in life and economic success for the country in which one grows up. As a result of this family relationships are increasingly overridden in favour of the working lives of both parents. So crèches and nurseries are geared towards 'education' and cognitive development. The emotional attachment needs of the children are systematically ignored, creating a high number of psychologically disturbed people who are unable to cope with life (Hüter, 2018).

Even if children lack for nothing in a material sense, if from an early age they have been passed from one out-sourced place of care to another they are the ones who suffer psychologically the most. Babies do not want to be in a crèche where they have to wait all day until they can be back with their mothers again (Sulz et al, 2018). Because this separation happens so early and goes on for so long, these children cannot develop a secure attachment with their mother and father; the foundation for solid psychological growth is not set up for them. They are internally in a state of constant stress (Grossmann and Grossmann, 2004), and are psychologically traumatised by the prolonged separation from their parents, forcing them to split off their feelings very early (Freund, 2014).

This raises the fundamental question as to why couples have children at all when, because of their situation in life, they do not have enough time and they cannot afford the required material resources, and often have no intrinsic interest in being there for the child to help them in their healthy growth. What is the point of bringing children into the world when, from the very beginning, we then want to get rid of them as often as possible, and neglect, threaten, punish and ultimately severely traumatise them?

Sexuality and Identity

The development of a healthy sexual identity: I = I

Who am I? What do I want? These are two basic questions when it comes to identity. Logically speaking, what is the truth and essence of identity? Why am I how I am?

I define identity as the sum of all our life experiences, everything that has happened to a person from the very beginning of his or her existence and how, as a subject, he/she reacts to those experiences. One's own life begins after a mother's egg cell has fused with a sperm cell from the father. The implantation in the uterus, the growth with placenta and umbilical cord, possible prenatal siblings, the birth preparation phase, the birth process itself, and the immediate time after birth are all important and formative experiences that, even though experienced unconsciously at an early age, all have a long-lasting effect in forming a person's personality. Based on my psychotherapeutic work, I am certain of that now. I have also clearly experienced it through my own personal therapeutic processes.

Identity is our physical and psychological existence, which primarily becomes real through feeling it. Healthy identity is the unconditional 'yes' to our own existence. At the beginning there is mere life force, the will to live and the zest for life. All this is not dependent on anything external, and therefore not on relationships. Healthy identity is a prerequisite for interpersonal relationships and for us to come into relationship with the world around us.

The formation of a conscious 'I' plays a central role in the development of our healthy identity. The 'I', as a reference point for our own development, is present from the beginning of our life. It is a special function of the human psyche that from the second year of life on becomes more and more conscious and can be easier and better expressed in words (Bauer, 2015). Only the person who can clearly feel his own 'I', and later also vocalise it,

Sexuality and Identity

is truly with himself. Because a human being is only one person with only one body, no two 'I's can exist side by side in a healthy psyche. Several 'I's existing simultaneously are a clear sign of a trauma-related psychological split. The inner world of such a person moves between several different levels of reality, of which one, at least, is illusionary and a trauma-surviving strategy, as the next example clearly shows.

Who am I?

Ruth had the following intention: "Ich will gesund ich sein" – Literal translation: "I want to be healthy I" (see Figure 1).

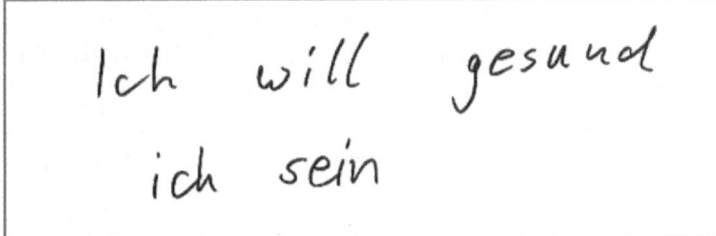

Figure 1

During this therapy process, it turned out that the second 'ich' ('I') became Ruth's father who had sexually traumatised her from when she was five until she left primary school. Ruth's mother already had three children and did not want Ruth, and offered her to her husband to fulfil his sexual needs right from the start. 'ich sein' ('to be I') was, for Ruth, synonymous with taking care of her father. In this way she could distract herself from her primary pain of not being wanted by her mother.

One's own healthy 'I' is the highest authority within the psyche of a non-traumatised person; there is nothing above. This 'I' cannot be replaced or transferred to any other person or institution. A healthy 'I' will not, for example, delegate responsibility for our own physical or psychological health to doctors or psychotherapists. Such people can only stand by our side and

35

help us in our process of self-healing with their skills, knowledge and good will. Conversely this also means that we cannot take on or claim responsibility for the 'I' of another person. Everyone is the supreme authority of their own psyche.

Identification: I = You

The concept of identity as I define it differs from the familiar notion that identity is to do with ancestry, roots and belonging. Seen from a logical perspective, this thinking makes the mistake of equating causes with conditions and circumstances. From my perspective there is a confusion here between the terms 'identity' and 'identification'. In a literal sense identity means something that equals with itself: $I = I$; there is the same quality on both sides of the equals sign and there is nothing extra or alien woven in it.

Identification on the other hand is the process by which someone, in his imagination, equates himself with someone or something outside of himself; so, I = you = my mother/my father/my siblings/my family/my birthplace/my home country/my football team/my job/my property and so on. This is a logical contradiction, which we can state as follows: I am what I am not, because it exists outside of me.

Given the multitude of opportunities to catalogue the circumstances of our own existence and identify with something external, it is no wonder that people really can't say exactly what belongs to their identity and what doesn't (Language? Eating habits? Religion? Culture? Land?) This false concept of identity becomes particularly confusing when the phenomena that a person identifies with have in themselves contradictory qualities:

- If at times a mother is loving, but more often she is hard and brutal.
- If the family you were born into did not really want you, but nevertheless finances your study.
- If the country with which you identify depicts itself as a protecting power, but at the same time sends you as a soldier into a war, and your own life is put on the line.

Identity = language?

Often reference is made to the common language in order to establish togetherness and solidarity as the basis for our own supposed identity. 'We' are, for example, 'German' (or English, or Italian, or Greek etc), because we all speak 'German' (English, or Italian or Greek etc). There is no doubt that the 'mother' language facilitates understanding amongst those who have learned this language. However, languages are just a means of communication, nothing more, and nothing less. Even within the state borders of the Federal Republic of Germany there are many dialects that are so different that, for example, people from the north of the country often find it difficult to have a conversation with those from the south.

If I would speak the dialect that is my mother tongue, few people would be able to understand me when I give lectures, talks or seminars. Therefore, I am glad to have mastered the High German language and English sufficiently to do my public and psychotherapeutic work.

In my opinion, it also depends on which of our internal parts is currently speaking. When we speak from the position of our healthy 'I' we use different words, concepts and sentence constructions than when we are speaking from the position of our psychotrauma survival strategies. There are particular syntax, semantics and pragmatics to the speech originating from a victim attitude, and another form of speech from the perpetrator attitude. It would be worthwhile researching this further through scientific studies.

The following example showed me how adhering to the dialect commonly spoken in the family had prevented the Intention Holder from becoming aware of the full scale of her sexual trauma.

Mother tongue = the language of the perpetrator

> *In a piece of IoPT work it struck me that the dialect of the Intention Holder was expressing an identification with her grandmother. The dialect with its clipped speech patterns, monosyllabic nature and fragmented sentences lent itself well to expressing victim and perpetrator attitudes, because it did not offer much means of communication, but rather represented depressive or aggressive utterances.*

Attributions: You = I

People who identify with their social and natural environment hold their symbiotic needs (desire for belonging, security and emotional support) in the foreground. Then those who wish to be identified with will exploit this need for their own purposes. They will support this misconception of identity, and ascribe to the people ideas of what they are supposed to be: You = someone who belongs to our culture, who abides by our morals, customs and laws, who does what we expect of them. It is obvious that those who promote this false idea of identity are also not clear themselves who they really are, and so it works to their advantage that the other person cannot clearly distinguish between "I" and "we". In this way, these exploiters of psychological confusion have an easy time carrying out their financial plans and power plays on dependent and subordinate people.

For me, the following example was a representation of patriarchal family relationships in its purest form: Man, Full-Stop and everything else (women and children) are trapped in it.

Sexuality and Identity

Who is 'I'?

Veronika's intention was 'Ich will bin.' / I want am. (Figure 2). Even the way it is written indicates that 'BIN' (AM) and 'WILL' (WANT) are trapped between the 'ICH' (I) and the 'full-stop' (.).

Figure 2: Wer ist ICH?

In the therapeutic process, it turned out that 'ICH'/'I' showed as Veronika's father, which indicated that Veronika had identified with him. Veronika had chosen a woman to resonate with this 'ICH'/'I', but the person resonating said she clearly felt male. This part had also stepped into the middle of the room right at the beginning of the process. The 'FULL-STOP' ('.') had then knelt in front of this resonator almost kissing her feet.

Veronika was the only child of her parents. Her mother did not really want children. Several pregnancies had ended in miscarriage before Veronika luckily survived her caesarean birth. She only existed because her father, in his patriarchal manner, insisted on his right to have children, no matter what the cost to his wife. Therefore, a part of Veronika admired her father. But she was blinded to the fact that she was only a means to prove his masculinity. In her life and in all her relationships with men, she had continued to practise this submissive attitude. Only during the process, in a conversation with the person resonating with 'BIN' ('AM'), did she become aware of this reality. Finally, crying, she began to feel the pain of being unwanted, unloved, and unprotected.

Comparison, differentiation, competition: I ≠ you

Anyone who seeks his identity by comparing himself to others ("Am I as good in bed as your last partner?", "Am I handsome enough?"), or by saying how he is different from them ("I never want to be like my mother/ my father! ") or is always trying to be better, faster, prettier, stronger ... than his fellow human beings (" I have the most beautiful breasts! ","I've got the biggest penis!"), fails to understand who he really is and what he could still become. By comparing, distancing or competing, our attention instantly goes away from ourselves and fixates on the outside world and on others.

Unfortunately, the element of competitiveness both within each gender and between men and women that is inherent in our sexual biology, fosters this global tendency. Whoever has to outdo or oust others in order to get the chance of having sex or reproducing is in a continual state of hypervigilance as to the plans and actions of others. He lives in constant fear that others might be stronger, better, faster or smarter, and thereby threaten his own status and rank as a sexual partner. Therefore, those living creatures that are currently in the alpha position are in a state of constant stress. This may be one reason why fewer men seek psychotherapeutic help than women, since they may fear that by looking within themselves they might be seen as weak and lose their status as a powerful and superior man. For this form of masculinity it is also the greatest violation, if their own wife has sex with another man, or perhaps has even shared a tender moment with them. To be a 'cuckold' in a patriarchal society is considered the greatest possible humiliation and dishonour. If a man's spouse is unfaithful, he may snap and have no qualms about beating or even killing her. On the other hand in patriarchal societies it is accepted as normal that men betray their women.

I am what I am not?

No man will become conscious of his own identity by wanting not to be like a woman. And no woman will discover her true identity by thinking she is more sensitive and emotional than a man. Heterosexual men will not understand themselves any better by saying "I'm not gay!" Sexual orientation in itself is only a part of a person's identity anyway.

The reason why it is even harder for men to live their true identity than it is for women is because, unfortunately, part of the stereotype of masculinity is to distance oneself from women by showing as few feelings as possible that could relate to their own inner reality ("I'm not a cry-baby" "All this psycho-babble is just for women"). If there are no real feelings, there is no real identity. Thinking alone creates only a twisted identity construction.

Defining your identity by what you are not can also lead to a depressive state of mind: I = no partner = no children = no money = no academic degree etc. It might be painful to miss something that you would like, but it does not mean this is your identity. Partners, children, financial wealth or academic degrees cannot fill up your inner emptiness. Anyone who does not have a connection to their own 'I', or had to give this up because of their traumatic life experiences, first has to re-establish contact with their 'I' within themselves. Only then can the external be included as something that actually enriches one's life. Relationships with other people are a supplement to, *not* a substitute for, one's own 'I'.

Sexual identity

In my experience people who stop comparing themselves, distancing themselves or competing with others, and instead begin to discover their own identity on the whole become more balanced, peaceful, and cooperative, and live healthier lives. Identity means knowing and understanding oneself: Who am I? What do I want in my life? These questions can only be answered if your own 'I' and your own 'want' were able to develop in the course of your life and were not given up in infancy because of early traumatisation (Ruppert and Banzhaf, 2018).

So what does identity mean ultimately in the context of our own sexuality? Regardless of whether I am in a female or male body, I must try to understand how my sexuality has developed from the beginning of my life. What barriers have been put in the way, and what has helped me to take on and live out my sexuality as part of who I am? Being physically a woman or a man is only the starting point from which to assert one's own subjectivity in all its uniqueness – and this includes one's sexuality.

Sexuality is being in one's body. If someone perceives his body as something unreal or strange, then the question has to arise: why? The fact that the psyche and body are already split from each other is, in my opinion, a consequence of trauma, and therefore requires clarification: how could such a thing happen?

Unless my development has been affected by psychotrauma, my sexuality can be part of me as a whole healthy organism, on a material, energetic and informational level:

- I am ...
- with my own want ...
- with my own feelings, ideas, thoughts and actions ...
- with my own needs ...
- in my body ...
- in contact with reality ...
- in constructive relationships.

When sexuality in this way is linked to identity it stops becoming merely about reproduction, quick sex or super-orgasms, or about behaving sexually in our relationship with our partner in order to keep them happy. Sexuality is not about gaining socially accepted status or even starting a family; it's about us humans as individuals, as subjects, and the main question is: Which forms of embodied sexuality promote a good life for oneself within a social community, and benefit everyone concerned, women, men and children?

What is 'normal' sexuality?

It is usually the case that men find women sexually attractive and vice-versa, and this is the driving force behind the sexual method of reproduction. However, it happens in all societies that some men find other men sexually attractive, or women fall in love with other women and want to have intimate contact with them. There are few reliable numbers about how common this is but the estimates vary between one and fifteen percent.

There are different opinions as to why people are attracted to someone of the same sex. Genes and hormones are considered as well as psychological development (Poiani, 2010). It is perhaps not surprising that women may feel physically attracted to other women as, when looking at this from a psychological perspective with the topic of early trauma in our thinking, they are unconsciously still searching for the love of and physical contact with their mother. Men in general tend to prefer women, who, perhaps like their mother, may give them closeness, security and physical affection. Why else would men find women's breasts so sexually irresistible? But it may also be that when a man finds another man attractive, he is unconsciously yearning for the fatherly love that he never received when he was a child.

Reproduction cannot take place through same-sex intimate contact, which is why conservative people portray homosexuality as unnatural, and morally and legally outlaw it. When someone points a finger at what they consider 'abnormal', they are also giving the seal of approval to what they consider normal, and are closed to any critical debate.

In modern Western societies, investigating the possible causes of homosexuality and other less common expressions of sexuality is currently viewed as politically incorrect, because of the possibility of discrimination. On the one hand, it is right that people should not be condemned and pathologised. No one should claim the right to inflict violence on others because of their sexual orientation or preferences, that are not part of the mainstream, as is unfortunately still the case in many countries worldwide. Some social groups are quick to scapegoat gay people to distract themselves from their own traumatised inner world and perpetrator actions, and so draw others into their perpetrator-victim dynamics (Amendt, 1979, p. 121ff.). Many of the problems that homosexual men and women face are as a result of being discriminated against as a social minority, so that the majority can feel 'normal' themselves, despite the huge extent of sexual trauma that exists generally within every 'normal' society between heterosexual women and men. In such ways wide spread psychotrauma survival strategies are stamped with the seal of 'normality'.

However it doesn't help if we make it a taboo to investigate the possible causes of sexual orientation and sexuality, thereby treating all sexual practices, whether heterosexual or gay, transgender, bisexual, as equally valid – regardless of how potentially degrading, painful, and shameful they may be for the people involved. Being gay, lesbian, bi, or trans may also be the consequence of having suffered childhood neglect, of being unloved, or of experiencing sexual traumatisation in childhood and adolescence, or even from having suffered rape in adulthood. One's own sexuality can function as a psychotrauma survival strategy to avoid coming into contact with perpetrators from the opposite sex, or it can be a restaging of the raw sexual violence or traumatising seduction situations that someone suffered as a child.

This is also true for heterosexual people; they can also abuse their sexuality in various ways as a distraction strategy from their trauma, using it to construct a pseudo-identity. Using sexual states of excitement and experiencing orgasms can for a while pacify their loneliness and inner emptiness. Extreme sexual practices associated with violence and pain, may be a repetition of perpetrator-victim relationships from early childhood. Risky sex, which carries the possibility of catching deadly infections, may be the expression of a death-wish that split off parts of the psyche have due to early traumatisation. Unfortunately traumatised societies tend to normalise psychotrauma, and this is nowhere more true than in the field of sexuality.

Artificial Insemination

Whether the booming business of artificial insemination and 'surrogate mothers' is indeed a 'normal' and acceptable solution for hetero- and homosexual couples who wish to have children and a family, must, in my view, also be subject to proper questioning from the perspective of trauma and survival strategies. Apart from the fact that poverty and illiteracy of young women is exploited, where surrogate mothers are recruited, for example in India or Latin America (Lenzen-Schulte, 2015), the question I have, from the perspective of attachment and trauma theory, is how the growing child in the womb experiences a mother who is contractually bound not to form a bond with them, and from whom the child is separated immediately after birth? How is it for the child if the fertilisation involves egg donation, and so the mother who incubates and gives birth to him is not genetically related to him? How does this child consciously and unconsciously deal with this situation when he later learns that he has two mothers, one genetic and one in whose belly he has spent the first months of his life? What is it like for the mother who does not see the child after delivery (stern.de, 2017)? How split off from herself and her feelings must she already be in order to be able to do this?

The use of multiple pregnancies, the prenatal killing of surplus 'embryos' and Caesarean deliveries in order to increase the success rate of artificial insemination raise further questions from a psychotrauma perspective that are empirically barely resolved. As is already well known in the case of adoption, the concealment of the child's origin is likely to lead to further psychological problems. In my practice every day I learn how much prenatal experiences leave a lasting mark on a person's psyche. Early psychological traumas have serious life-long consequences (Ruppert, 2015).

Transgender

On the subject of transgender,[5] some people see the tendency of a child to feel that they belong to the opposite sex as just another variant of sexuality that should not be pathologised and, even that they should be encouraged to change their body by hormonal or surgical measures (WDR, 2017). Others warn against ignoring the possible psychological background of a troubled gender identity (Preuss, 2016). In my opinion, people with a 'trans-' sexual orientation should be encouraged to look into possible trauma causes in their biography before embarking on chemical and surgical routes, and undergoing an operation to transition from one gender to the other: Why do I have these ideals of masculinity or femininity in my mind? Why do I feel particularly attracted by them, even though my body does not correspond to these ideals about gender? Why do I reject my body, and even consider cutting off my genitals or breasts?

There is much technically and hormonally possible these days, but operations like these are traumatic, at the very least physically, and only lead to a physical gender reassignment. Administered sex hormones give rise to artificial, externally produced bodily and emotional experiences that stop, if the hormones are stopped. Whether or not attachment disorders or psychotrauma are the cause of the alien-from-yourself feeling in your own body should, in my view, be thoroughly and carefully looked into, with the following hypotheses as worth considering,

- The parents wanted a child of a different gender.
- The parents had previously lost a child of the opposite gender, and had not sufficiently mourned the loss.
- Because of their own sexual trauma a mother may unconsciously give the unborn children the message: "It's not right that you are a boy/a girl."
- Or there can be a symbiotic entanglement with a twin of the opposite sex who died early in the womb.

Only a few people come to me directly because of their sexual orientation. In the following case study the young woman had been persuaded by her worried mother to have an individual session with me, rather than really wanting to do it herself.

I want to cut off my breasts

In a therapy session with a very self-conscious young woman, who wanted to have her breasts cut off so that she could become a boy, I got the impression that she wanted to have this primary symbol of motherliness taken away so that she could try to differentiate herself from her dominant mother, with whom she had no emotional connection and against whom she could not compete rationally. Because of this, I told her that in my opinion it would help her substantially in the development of her identity if, instead of cutting off her breasts, she first cuts the umbilical cord with her mother that still exists psychologically. Unfortunately, she has not turned up for another appointment since.

Sexuality and Society

Sexuality and traditional societies

In the 21st Century, because of globalisation, human societies that have for thousands of years developed independently now directly clash with each other over their different value systems in regards to sexuality. This results in many conflicts and leads to traditional and modern sexual practices existing side by side and in opposition to each other, sometimes in the most confined of spaces. The social aspect of sexuality is not only about attitudes and about behaviours that are handed down from one generation to the next, it is also about the political power and economic interests that are linked to the sexuality and sexual needs of the members of the society. Through laws, moral rules or religious dogma, every society tries to somehow control the potential anarchy of sexual desire.

Did Eve tempt Adam and thereby get their divine paradise taken away from them both, as the bible preaches? Or is it really men, who, with their sexual libidos, incessantly pursue women and make their lives a hell? Since the world religions are a product of their male founders, they interpret female sexuality from the perspective of male sexual interests. It is often claimed that a woman's sexuality is excessively hungry, insatiable and dirty. Men have to beware of it and restrict and control it, otherwise they may fall under its spell and no longer be able to lead a godly life. It is women's sexuality and their propensity for infidelity that endangers the 'honour' of men. Fear of menstrual blood, the obsession with virginity, chastity belts and female genital mutilation are amongst the many consequences of this way of thinking. If a woman is raped, it is not she who is the victim, but the man to whom she 'belongs.' She is the actual perpetrator, who then has to be put in the stocks, flogged or stoned. Since Freud (1856-1939) this psychological mechanism has been called 'projection': I transfer my own psychological

Sexuality and Society

structures onto my opponent. They then appear to me to be the perpetrator and I the victim. In truth, however, I am the perpetrator and I make others the victim of my unresolved internal conflicts.

Patriarchal societies

The religious reading of female sexuality goes hand in hand with the society-wide dominance of men, in whose hands rest material ownership, economic disposal and military means of violence. In patriarchal societies, men believe that they have a claim on women's bodies and may use them to satisfy their sexual needs whenever they wish. That is why, in such societies, men acquire the right of ownership to women and children through marriage. 'Strong' men, who because of sexual stereotyping have become unsympathetic and unfeeling, protect the 'weak' women, who are supposedly drowning in their feelings. In these societies, arranged marriages and rules of dowry enforce the subjugation of marriageable children no matter how young they are, according to what is dictated by the male head of the family.

Here, men also hold onto the right to lash out if they become sexually frustrated. This can then deepen into a fury and a jealousy that knows no bounds that can come out against their wives and just as easily against their children. They show no consideration and blindly ruin whatever is around them. They do not understand that this makes them more and more isolated and that hardly anyone still loves them willingly or sincerely, because they stubbornly refuse to deal with their own psyche. For men shaped by patriarchy, their image of women is split: there are the 'sainted Madonnas' – their own mother, the unattainable lover – and also there are 'whores' – all those women who can be raped with impunity.

Women adapt to these conditions as best they can. The following testimonial from a widowed woman in India is characteristic of patriarchal societies: "If you are alone as a woman, many men believe they can treat you badly. I have a male neighbour who often harasses me. It is really unpleasant. I wish my husband were still with me. Even if he was an alcoholic or knocking about with other women, it would still be better than not having a husband."[6]

Because of their trauma these women have had to give up contact with themselves early on, and so feel weak and powerless and look for support from outside of themselves. Since the majority of women around them are also weak and oppressed, they find little help amongst other women. In such societies the only strength a woman can find is the apparent strength of men. Although these men are perpetrators, because internally they are weak and insecure, they appear to women as saviours and protectors. From a female perspective, it seems logical then to orient oneself to the strongest and most powerful man. Daughters, too, have little inducement to take on their mother as a role model, as she is subordinate to the father. Even her brothers are more respected by her mother than she is. The mother admires her sons, since the birth of a son affords the woman a higher status than a daughter does, and they often experience daughters as a burden.

In the order of a patriarchal society, mothers manipulate their children to fit in with their own trauma survival strategies. She imposes on her children traditional gender roles from which she herself cannot break free. Against the totalitarian grip maintained by both parents, children have little chance of developing their own vision for life, never mind developing their own sexuality. Their entire psychological experience is monopolised by a traumatised father and a traumatised mother who, looked at in terms of psychological maturity, are still children themselves. The children's own feelings, thoughts and development of identity are therefore nearly impossible to develop in this social setup.

A particularly drastic example of this social prison is societies that persist in genital mutilation of girls. To become a 'real woman' girls must have their clitoris and/or the outer and inner labia cut off with a razor blade, knife, or some other sharp-edged object. They are told that only if they are so circumcised, can they be deemed respectable, and stand a chance of getting a man who will marry them, and have children. The 'circumcision' is often performed in the presence of the child's own mother, aunts and grandmothers. This process, which is shocking in its insanity and savagery, is justified by the parents because otherwise the woman would be deemed sexually insatiable and likely to be unfaithful to her husband. The psychological and physical consequences of these genital mutilations are atrocious. If the child survives this procedure at all, which is dependent upon the extent of the circumcision, she will endure a lifetime of permanent pain when urinating, having sexual intercourse, menstruating or giving birth. They will end up no longer able to trust anyone and, later, they themselves may become callous perpetrators to their own daughters (Javakhidze, 2018).

Even though it may cause less severe physical consequences, genital cutting of male babies and small boys will still have severe psychological consequences, with the more or less radical removal of the foreskin that covers and protects the glans of the penis. This procedure is likewise part of traditional patriarchal societies, and has consequences for boys, who because of the traumatised community into which they are born, will have little chance of a healthy sexual development, physically or psychologically. Even in 'enlightened communities' there is still a tolerance for such cultural and religious principles, so that young boys are helplessly surrendered to the garbled ideas of their parents, relatives and religious leaders, and are systematically sexually traumatised. I have witnessed men who have explored their circumcision in a therapy session, and have seen how painful and humiliating this process was for them.

Within the framework of my psychotrauma theory patriarchy is the social expression of male perpetrator attitudes as a trauma survival strategy. The shame and physical and mental pain of men are transformed into aggression and lack of feeling, to keep their own victimhood at bay. Men generally become trauma perpetrators when they have been trauma victims before. This is almost without exception the case in most societies. Those men are born and raised by traumatised mothers who cannot give them real love because they themselves are split from their feelings. The psyche of such boys is traumatised from a very early age. They are then full of fear, suppressed anger, false concepts and illusions of love. Female victim-attitudes, which prevent women from confronting the reality of their own traumatisation, flourish in a patriarchal society, and so the whole society exists in a vicious self-perpetuating cycle, which is passed on from generation to generation.

Where religion maintains the position of a state ideology, as for example used to be the case in medieval Europe, or as is currently the situation in strict Islamic countries, in Orthodox Judaism or in the American Bible Belt, the whole of sexuality is defined as impure and disgusting. Any form of sexuality outside of marriage, within which it is only permitted for reproductive purposes, is branded as ungodly, unchaste, a sin and a crime, and may be punished by incarceration, flogging, being put in stocks or banishment from societies where this is permitted by law. There exists an almost manic preoccupation with 'adultery', 'being unchaste' or 'being a whore' as a means to ensure a God-fearing, pious society (Dabhoiwala, 2014). Anyone who tries to break away from such a coercive society is threatened with contempt and eternal damnation.[7]

Matrilineal Societies

Very few traditional societies are not organised along patriarchal lines. In these matrilineal communities (including the Hopi Indians in North America, the Minangkabau in West-Sumatra and the Mosuo in China), women do not become a man's property through partnership or marriage. In such communities they do not inevitably walk right into the poverty trap because they are not automatically economically dependent on a man when they have children. In some societies it is of no importance as to who the father of the child is. Women select their lovers, and both lead a 'visit-based relationship'. With the Mosuo, for example, the men continue to live in their mother's clan house, and participate in the education of the children of their sisters and of the mother's sisters, and make themselves useful as general labour force for the group (Coler, 2010). Sexuality is lived out in a discreet way.

Dagmar Margotsdotter, who met the people of the Mosuo while visiting Lake Lugu in China, describes them as follows: "They are relaxed, healthy and happy, caring and considerate of each other, modest about themselves and benevolent towards each other. They do not suffer from stress, obesity, anorexia or other addictions like many of us [in the west], nor from competition or isolation, greed or jealousy." (Margotsdotter, 2016, p. 280).

In matrilineal societies there is a strong feeling of 'we' in the mother clan, and this is kept alive through ancestral cults and the natural religion's references to motherhood, and is passed on to the next generation by many rituals.

Since ethnicities recognised by the Chinese state as minorities must be available for tourism, such contact between tourists and locals makes the differences between patriarchal and matriarchal people very obvious. As footage shows (Madeisky et al, 2014) the tourist groups are without boundaries and are sensation seeking. The male tourists are clearly intrusive and sexualised in their behaviour towards the females of the Mosou.

In patriarchal societies women, and therefore mothers, are systematically traumatised, and this leads to an extreme lack of healthy mothering for the children (Maaz, 2005). This in turn, in my view, is the reason for the hyper-sexualisation that is commonplace in patriarchal societies. Emotionally frustrated children try to make up for their lack of mothering through sexual contact as adolescents and adults. This endeavour is always in vain and leads to sexual addictions and the further sexual traumatisation of others in such patriarchal societies.

Sexuality and modern societies

As the separation of state and religious authority began to happen in some European countries from the 18th Century onwards, the process was also supported on an intellectual level. The Enlightenment encouraged people to think for themselves and not be subordinate to religious dogma. Humanists, at least on an intellectual level, removed the equation 'God = man' from the centre of life. Instead, they put the individual human being at the centre. They saw human need, and therefore sexuality, as something natural; as long as it did no harm to others, it should be available to anyone as a source of pleasure and joy, and so it should not be restricted by laws or moral concepts. Even if men were to have sex with men or women had sex with women, it was ultimately their own private affair that the state or the church should not interfere with. The state should only appear on the scene if there were good grounds given to limit the sexuality of their members, for example when it came to the prohibition of non-consensual sex, as with rape or under-age sex with children. In the field of sexuality, every fully-grown adult should be the architect of his own fortune.

However, even societies that from 19th through to 21st centuries have constitutionally prescribed and still prescribe the ideals of 'liberty, equality and fraternity', have not abolished the status quo of political and economic balance of power, but only shifted it within the ranks of society. In principle now, everyone can fight against everyone else for status and influence, but the male rivalry for power and possessions remains upheld and, freed from religious imperatives, class barriers and moral caveats, it now becomes the driving force for social development. In place of God we now have self-propagating money (capital), which is to be worshipped and revered, as the mythical golden calf was once idolised (Senf, 2004). The 'market' and the idea of unending 'growth' become a substitute religion around which all the thoughts and energies of the members of nationally organised states revolve. The majority of people only shifted from moral obedience and dependency on religious leaders to wage dependency on employers and the ideological devotion to politicians who want to keep these social conditions running, despite the many miseries that come as a result.

In addition, the members of such competitive communities are subtly but constantly policed by the editors-in-chief of the public media to see members of other nation states as competi-

Sexuality and Society

tors for economic goods and, if necessary, as potential enemies against which war will have to be waged, which is always the case due to the ever-present national conflicts of interest. Men then go to war with the idea of safeguarding their wives and children from the enemies on the other side of the state border fences when in fact they only help capitalism to become more and more global.

Against this background, the question arises as to how free sexuality actually is in modern society. Sexuality is now another means of personal fulfilment in the competition of everyone against everyone else, and, on top of that, it seems that the cost and benefits of a sexuality freed from religious and moral dogma continue to be unevenly distributed between men and women. The role of a woman is still to sexually satisfy a man. Whether she feels this desire herself is rather beside the point. Many women count themselves lucky if they at least do not feel pain during sex. The task of emotional comfort and encouragement in everyday struggles is delegated to women. Men cover up their frustrated desire for closeness and satisfaction of their sexual needs by constantly working on their competitive projects. Even in our modern societies boys and girls are still, from an early age, attributed gender roles. For example, pink is considered the colour for girls, and blue for boys. Girls play with dolls, boys with diggers and guns. Girls play with skipping ropes, boys climb trees. Girls will later become nurses, boys engineers. Girls are conditioned to look pretty and please men. Boys should be big and strong in order to be impressive to women.

With economic competition, competitiveness between the sexes is fuelled. Men see women as rivals for the scarce opportunities for earning ('the workplace'). In addition, women, when they do get an employment contract, are usually easier to exploit than men. The needs of children to spend time with their parents, and the possibility of parents having sufficient time to look after the welfare of their children properly, fall victim to the relentless market economy laws of wage labour.

So it comes as no surprise that many women question their role as mothers and prefer to fulfil themselves in their professional life instead. The 'emancipation of women' inevitably calls for state-run third-party care of children. So the French feminist. Elisabeth Badinter, criticises "women who breastfeed their children or who wish to stay at home substantially longer than the state-recommended ten weeks after birth. Such a 'return to naturalism' serves only to bind women to the hearth." (Finkenzeller, 2019, p. 47) The needs of children are, as always in the history of humankind, overlooked, disregarded and trampled underfoot (Fuchs, 2019).

Sexuality becomes a commodity and through its commercialisation great profits can be made:

- With the promise of making your body sexually attractive and more successful than the competition, multi-billion profits are made in the fashion, cosmetics and plastic surgery industries.
- Presenting your partner as a showpiece and object of prestige, whilst you continue to climb your own career ladder, is common in capitalistic societies. Success is seen as sexy, and being sexy makes you successful.
- Gender stereotypes are built into and marketed in the media to maximise profits and 'efficiency' in the commercial economic system. Product advertising reflects the current roles of men and women.
- 'Fertility Centres' make a lot of money by selling hopes of domestic happiness for the many couples who cannot achieve parenthood naturally.
- Because it is potentially a lucrative business, research is now conducted so that two egg cells can be fertilised in order to fulfil a lesbian couple's desire for each to have a child without a sperm cell from a man.
- The prostitution and pornography industries exploit unsatisfied sexual desires and porn addiction in psychologically sophisticated and shameless ways. In the age of the Internet, their clientele are offered previously undreamt of opportunities, which are converted into profits in the billions.

- With IT technology, sex toys are being created which become ever more human-like, and more expensive to buy.

Nonetheless, the idea of marriage and family, which is oriented towards traditional gender roles, continues to be regarded as the nucleus of a national state. This ensures that through foster care for babies and toddlers, sufficient women are available for the competitive business economy. Nurseries, where infants of just a few months old are given into the hands of overburdened nursery educators for eight hours or more a day, are then extolled as progressive (Ballmann, 2019). Women who want to take care of their children for longer are disparaged as 'clingy mothers', so as to have as many women as possible available as a work-force. Even in modern industrial societies, women with children, despite all statements about the 'advancement of women', are at a higher risk of poverty and, despite social welfare systems, continue to live on the breadline, even after reaching retirement age. Economic power continues to be male-dominated, and even if women do the same job they are generally paid less than men.

Political power is still largely held by men, who carry their competitiveness to extremes. Women who go into the economy and politics subordinate themselves to the rules of male competitive behaviour. In all competitive societies, women are still expected to produce offspring for the nation, for the economy, for the military, for the welfare systems. A participant in my seminars in England recalled a Victorian saying to the effect that women who did not want sex with their husband were told, "to lie back and think of England."

Presumably the pill, that reliable hormonal contraception for women which has been available since 1960, has contributed the most to the sexual liberalisation of many societies in the world. In addition, romantic ideals of everlasting love, loyalty and family have become questioned with the availability of sexual partners via dating portals. 'Friendship with benefits' is the modern buzzword for those who yearn for sex but don't want to enter into a permanent relationship and produce children.

Whether that works out well or ends up in the chaos of jealousy and desire for love and binding partnership, everyone has to find out for themselves. To beget and raise children increasingly becomes a more conscious decision, with all the associated doubts and conflicts between men and women.

Sexuality, Fascism & Totalitarianism

In the thinking of the far right, the myth of the strong, invincible man is carried to its extreme. Even in modern societies, bound up in the competition between nations, this mentality can easily tip into political fascism and is widely spread as the base for the military systems. Adolf Hitler said during his speech in Nuremberg in 1935 that the Hitler Youth should be "slim and agile, swift as greyhounds, tough as leather and hard as Krupp Steel" (Roddewig, 2012). An absolute lack of feeling and total military obedience is postulated as the ultimate ideal of men. Fear, pain or compassion cannot hold a place in a totally de-personalised male psyche. Supposed weaknesses must be mercilessly suppressed vigorously in both oneself and others. One's own body must function like a machine made of steel, constantly achieving top performance. The fascist man becomes the instinct-driven killer. He attempts to totally merge his 'I' in the identification with the idea of a racially pure people. He is both overbearing and submissive. His lust is sadistic and masochistic in turn.

Within this context, military and imperial attitudes are transferred onto sexual relationships. Fighting engenders lustful feelings, and sex becomes part of the battle for existence. Women are there to salute men for their warlike heroism and reward them by making themselves available for sex. The fascist worldview appeals to the supposed law of nature that only the strongest will survive. It can therefore only be one person who stands at the top of the social hierarchy. Anyone who pulls this off is justifiably the all-powerful and infallible 'leader'. He must be worshipped like a god. Below him, there are the sub-leaders with their own respective acolytes, who may behave in a similar holier-than-thou way.

Parties who call themselves 'communist' can also pedal to people this male-fantasy of absolute power and control, elevated to a state ideology. The result of men claiming the form of power that takes no responsibility for themselves and their traumatised psyches is predictable, with well-known consequences of war, chaos, destruction, oppression, lies and deceit.

In addition to this principle of the all-powerful father figure as the highest head of state, an ideal of the mother is propagated that can be fulfilled by giving birth to children for the totalitarian state. In the time of fascist German imperialism Johanna Haarer (1934) wrote in her guidebook for women, 'The German Mother and her first child' of how mothers ought to deal with their children: no bodily contact, no love, toughening up and frustration of the child's needs – hence the systematic engendering of attachment trauma from the beginning. Wherever the capitalistic economy becomes predominant the needs of unborn children and babies for maternal love do not count at all.

Biologically being a mother, in this way of thinking, is already an honour in itself. Any form of more loving motherliness is out of place. Therefore the child must worship his mother, solely because she gave birth to him. The same applies to the father: He is the producer of the child and that is enough and we must be ever grateful to him for that. The 'gift of life' is to be accepted whatever the cost: everyone must at the same time be willing to sacrifice his own life in the fight for 'The People', for 'God's own Country', 'The King' or 'The Fatherland' or the 'Glorious revolutionary Party'. Marriage and family stand in service to the national community, which is in a constant state of competition and war with the countries that surround it. In addition, totalitarian institutions are created that stifle any individuality and subjectivity before it gets a chance to develop. There is no official leeway for lustful sexuality and tender love. When needed state brothels are set up for the soldiers in wars to discharge their mechanical impulses. The rape of the 'enemy's' women is an unspoken tactic of war and is politically encouraged or at least silently condoned.

The trauma survival strategy of seeking by every means to

totally control a person's inner life and the outer world is taken to a further extreme by the current technological revolution. What George Orwell described back in 1948 as a dystopia in his novel *1984* has now become more and more true. 'Big Brother is watching you' has become a reality everywhere with installed cameras and spyware in our computers and smart phones. In this way states and economic cartels aim to have total access to the private life of every one of us, allowing them to manipulate our psyches thereby retaining power and the freedom to collectively generate and acquire their own private wealth (Mausfeld, 2018).

If you take a quick look at the biographies, the childhood and adolescent histories, of the men who rule at the head of the most powerful and most weaponised nations on the globe in 2019 (Donald Trump, Vladimir Putin and Xi Jinping), you look into an abyss where there is no love, only neglect; where there are lots of physical experiences of violence and psychological humiliations (Lee, 2018; Fuchs, 2019). What disasters would be spared us if our political leaders were psychologically mature human beings, who could stay in peace with themselves instead of inflicting fear and terror by transferring their trauma survival strategies onto the entire world, re-enacting their terrible childhood experiences? Anyone who threatens nuclear war is potentially also considering suicide. That deeply traumatised people have made it to such powerful positions, with millions of supporters behind them, is for me the greatest evidence of how traumatised and traumatising the societies are that these people lead.

One of my fundamental beliefs is this: a person who faces his own painful psychological realities could not be a totalitarian, or even an authoritarian. He would not bring into being or take on the running of any system that brings misery, enslavement and death to the majority of people. He does not need external enemies in order to distract himself from his internal terror. If he can begin to have compassion for himself, he can have it for others; he can clearly distinguish between being a victim and being a perpetrator – both within himself and in the outside world (Ruppert, 2019).

Sexuality and Society

Sexuality, Culture & Migration

I'd like to begin this section with my own experiences.

Citizens and Foreigners

I was born in 1957 in a little Franconian village in Germany. There were never any informative conversations about sexuality in my family, but the subject of sex was all-pervasive during family get-togethers, especially from the men, who would liberally throw it into the conversation in the form of dirty stories, jokes and insinuations. As alcohol consumption increased, the conversations would take a turn for the worse.

Back then, the underwear and bra section of the Neckermann mail-order catalogue was the only way I could see a woman's naked body. During puberty I suffered considerably from wet dreams; and then the question arose: what was I to do with my pyjama bottoms, with the wet spots so clearly visible? How depraved was I already then? Did I have to confess every Saturday to the village priest all the unclean thoughts that came into my mind day and night?

At that time there were only a few cars about, and bigger distances could only be covered on foot or by bike. Even in the village two kilometres down the road, the dialect had a slightly different sound. When we were invited to family and church festivals in a nearby village, the other children and young people would invite me to play football with them. As I grew older my interest 'naturally' turned to the local village beauties. But what I could do with these women was not clear to me. Did they just want a boyfriend so they could say they were now 'going out' with someone? Or did they, like me, yearn for sexual satisfaction? Or did they want me to marry them and start a family? Luckily my first girlfriend was already sexually experienced, and could enjoy sex; her parents were relatively liberal and we were allowed to spend the night together in their house.

Later, as a student, I went on my first trips to Italy, in the hope of meeting young Italian women, who were considered by my circle of friends to be particularly beautiful and desirable. I had a less good opinion of Scandinavian and American women tourists because they were considered too liberal, and so I was on guard against them. During this time, I defined myself in relationship to women as follows: if they found me attractive that made me feel good; if they ignored me I felt bad. A good-looking girlfriend by my side seemed like the fulfilment of all my dreams. Look here, everyone, at what a great man I must be, because I have conquered such a beautiful woman! My religious mother's influence on me was not big enough to discourage premarital sex. Liberal thinking was already so widespread at that time, that we young people were able to have a more relaxed attitude towards our sexuality, in spite of our conservative parents.

My first big trip around the world in 1974 took my girlfriend and me to Tunisia and Algeria. There I experienced the blatant harassment of my blonde-haired female companion by men of all ages. I soon began to feel like her 'minder', who could not allow her out of his sight. When we were invited to a traditional wedding celebration with highly covered and veiled women in an Algerian oasis, we were amazed at the number of young men who had studied in Paris and Hanover and were now back home for the holidays. They portrayed themselves as very liberal and enlightened. One even had several pithy sayings such as "Pour moi le couple n'existe pas!" ("For me the couple relationship does not exist!") This sounded almost like the German Student movement of 1968, right here in the depths of the Algerian desert. "Whoever sleeps with the same person twice is already part of the establishment!"[8] We were even more disillusioned when one of them tried to entice my girlfriend away from me under some pretext, in order to rape her. I experienced that as a deep betrayal of trust, and we left this place as fast as possible.

For a long time, the issue of male violation of others did not personally concern me until, in 2015, millions of fleeing people sought asylum in Germany. I could not imagine that this situation would go well for very long when you had predominantly many unmarried men in the sexually active phase of their life with a traditional picture of women in their heads arriving in Germany.

Young men who think that women, who go about on their own, are fair game, unless they are protected by a man. What happened in the cathedral square in Cologne on New Year's Eve in 2015 has confirmed this fear, as groups of male asylum seekers surrounded women, insulted, and severely sexually molested them.

The highly emotionally charged asylum debate that has raged in Germany since 2015 has many causes (Palmer, 2017). One thing is that German men fear that their wives and children cannot be adequately protected from immigrant foreign men. Therefore, any incident in which an asylum seeker touches a German woman against her will, rapes, or even kills her will cause major outrage. German women also fluctuate between their humanitarian impulse to help the migrant women, mothers and children in their hour of need, and their distrust of the men whose behaviour they find difficult to assess and who are often openly hostile to German women. They also want the newly arrived women to emancipate themselves from their traditionally subordinate attitude as quickly as possible, hence the heated debates about headscarves and veils.

However covering-up and disguising yourself are easily understandable protective strategies in a world in which women are hounded by sex-obsessed men (and this applies not only to Islamic societies). However, this strategy of hiding away only works to a certain extent, and does not work at all if the perpetrator happens to live where the woman's only safe haven is: her own home. However if the 'covering-up' is seen in connection with its true cause, rather than as justified by a higher authority (for example, as an expression of religion or culture) then it is more likely to be understood as a trauma survival strategy: as a woman I am not allowed to be aware of the real threat or perceive myself as a victim; I dare not allow myself to clearly identify and name the perpetrators. Then I go into a seemingly self-imposed submissive attitude, and put shame on myself in front of the perpetrator. So, if you try to take away this trauma survival strategy (the covering-up) the victims of sexual violence will fight against it, so long as they do not feel safe from male attacks, even in the home.

Theories of Sexuality and Society

Since the theme of sexuality is a highly social issue, enlightened psychological theories on the topic have a certain explosive power for the status quo. This was the experience of Sigmund Freud, for example, whose theory of sexuality was first met with scepticism, but also with great interest from many of his contemporaries. However, when he ventured deeper into the hornet's nest of the sexual abuse of children within the family, he himself drew back out of fear that he would be socially marginalised; subsequently he rescinded these discoveries in favour of what was then called 'hysteria'. He toned down and falsified his insights to the detriment of his patients, saying instead that the sexual traumatisation of these children had not really happened, and that it was the natural sexual development of the child to have fantasies of wanting to have sex with and marry their opposite gender parent. This in Freud's opinion led to the accounts of dreams of being sexually assaulted by their parents (Freud, 1972). Moreover, for Freud the suppression of instinctual sexuality (sublimation) was at the root of cultural achievements, and as such a good and necessary psychological act. As a result of these theories he became again an honourable member of the bourgeois community after his death.

Wilhelm Reich (1897-1957) saw it differently. His critical attitude towards society addressed directly the issue of sexuality, suggesting that the suppression of the working class had its origin in the suppression of their sexuality. As Reich saw it, there was direct correlation between this suppression of sexuality and the development of authoritarian forms of government, especially fascism (Reich, 1971). Sex education was for him synonymous with a revolution in favour of a classless society of free and creative people. He saw that people's bodies had become hardened because of the blocking of feelings, and that by having as good an orgasm as possible this hard shell would become superfluous, thereby allowing people to become more relaxed and peaceful.

Alfred Kinsey (1894-1956) originally catalogued the development of gall wasps before turning his attention to the exploration of human sexuality. He broke the taboo, and was the first person to ask American men questions about their sex lives. What he brought to light about sexual practices, and how widespread they were, astonished the public. When he afterwards questioned American women, and demonstrated that they too were anything but the idealised creatures of American Puritanism, he came under considerable pressure from the American public insitutions, both as a university professor and as a private individual. Yet his publication of his interviews ('The Kinsey Report') is still considered a milestone in the liberalisation of human sexuality (Boyle, 2019).

The 1968 student revolutionary movement, which seized many European countries, as well as Japan and America, subscribed to the writings of Wilhelm Reich and his idea that the transformation of prevailing economic and political conditions must be accompanied by a liberation from sexual constraints and norms. Communes were set up that practised 'free love' without the constraint of fixed partnerships. The institute of marriage was discredited and sex education was seen as part of the political fight for individual liberties against authoritarian structures (Amendt, 1979).

The book by Hans-Joachim Maaz, 'The New School of Lust' (Maaz, 2017) is a sex education book in its best sense. He explains the basic physical and psychological dimensions of desire, connecting issues of physical lust and the desire for relationship in an easy to understand way, thanks to his extensive experience as a psychotherapist. He points out how social structures both cause and maintain a disruption of our lusts and desires for relationships, and goes on to say that there is an emancipatory potential in a sexuality that is aligned with a person's identity.

We have come a long way from the concept of hysteria of the 19th century to the uninhibited granting of pleasurable sensations for both genders that we have reached at the beginning of the 21st century. While Freud said that vaginal orgasm was the pinnacle of fulfilment for women, even though three-quarters of women do not reach climax during vaginal intercourse, it is now scientifically accepted that the primary source of sexual gratification for women is through clitoral stimulation. The biology of the sexual organs of both sexes has been clarified scientifically, and the psychological taboos and the barriers of shame surrounding sex are largely overcome.

Theories of sexuality as discussed in most Western countries today are more influenced by sociological ideas. While the word 'sex' refers to whether a person is physically male or female, the term 'gender' serves to address what culturally and socially shapes a person's sexuality. Gender role behaviour and role expectations in social groups are directly connected to sexuality. Increasingly in these discourses body and psyche are seen as completely separate entities: anyone born in a male body should still be able to lead a woman's life if he wants to, and vice versa. The adjustment of a body to fit the psychological desire to be a woman or a man is seen as the manifestation of the highest form of individual freedom. Since modern medicine can provide the necessary techniques to achieve such gender reassignment, it now seems to only be a question of personal choice as to which gender identity somebody wants to live. In addition, society is urgently called upon to put in place the appropriate infrastructures to enable everyone to live out their own diverse sexual orientation (for example separate toilets for intersexuals and transsexuals). The focus of this discourse then leads to the question: who discriminates against and stigmatises whom based on his sexual orientation (Nunez and Schneeberger, 2018).

In my opinion, the discourse about gender often causes more confusion than clarity, because as previously referred to, in my experience the separation of the body and the psyche is already a result of a trauma of identity. To explore this fact in more detail in oneself might be far more useful for those concerned than losing themselves further within rational and ideological discussions that dissociate even more from one's own body.

Basic risks for the development of sexuality

Biological failures – Intersexuality

Human sexuality is threatened by potential risks to its development on all levels, biological, psychological and societal. For example, the sexual organs may not develop sufficiently or correctly, or there could both be ovaries and testes developing in one body termed 'sexual hermaphroditism' or 'intersex'. This generic term includes a large number of diagnoses, the common denominator being that the characteristics that define females or males – chromosomes, genes, hormones, gonads, and external sex organs – do not correspond clearly to one specific sex (Stüvel, 2008). This is estimated to occur in one out of every 10,000 people, and leads to demands to legally establish a 'third gender'. However, the decision is often taken by doctors or parents to make the child's sexuality unequivocally clear through surgery while they are still a baby, without the consent of the child. In my view it is better to allow the person themselves to make the decision as to how they want to deal with this feature of their body. The pressure from outside to choose one gender is not helpful for living your own identity even if it is experienced as a handicap.

Psychological immaturity

The development of sexuality can also be limited psychologically and remain stuck at a certain developmental stage (prenatal, early or late childhood, puberty, adulthood or older). A boy is unable to become a man, remaining arrested in his childhood state, the term 'Peter Pan' syndrome has been adopted to describe this. Also, when a woman gets stuck at the stage of being a little girl, this is quickly obvious in her childlike behaviour. Reasons for this can be:

- that parents have kept these children dependent and unable to fend for themselves;
- that childhood sexual trauma occurred;

- that sexually traumatised parents unconsciously convey the message to their children: "Whatever else you do, do not become a man/woman, because then you will become a sexual perpetrator/victim".

In western societies children often receive the message from adults that only youthfulness is attractive and growing up is not really worth it.

Ideological barriers

Within many societies, sexual taboos, myths and ideologies still function to ensure that its members remain sexually raw and primitive. If sexuality is a topic that is not spoken about and not allowed to be practised before marriage then for many people it comes as a nasty surprise on their wedding night. The man may have no idea of his wife's anatomy or emotional needs and cannot bring her to sexual climax. She, in turn, experiences sexual intercourse as an act of violence, which is unsatisfying and not pleasurable for him either. In this way sexual intercourse is stuck at an animalistic level.

The pressure from society to claim the 'virginity' of an unmarried woman is due to the misconception that the 'hymen' would be pierced by her husband's penis on the wedding night and then bleed. As proof of her virginity, the relatives must be presented with the blood-stained bed sheets the following morning. However, the folds of skin that are located at the end of the vaginal passage, and are medically termed as the 'hymen', are not a seal over the uterus, which would then have to be opened like a kind of keep-fresh lid. This is completely nonsensical because how then could the menstrual blood flow out? The first sexual intercourse that a woman has can cause bleeding, but it does not have to. It depends on the sensitivity with which the man carries out the sexual foreplay and introduces his penis into her vagina (Brochmann and Støkken Dahl, 2018, p. 29 ff.). The extreme of this sexual ideology is shown in offers to surgically rebuild the 'hymen' by doctors.

The world is upside down and everything is warped when in a society, women who have been raped are labelled as 'whores' and are ostracised. When they themselves are accused of seducing their rapists and of soiling the family honour (Sanyal, 2016). In some places women are even stoned for it. In patriarchal societies the perpetrators of trauma cover for each other and the women keep silent in fear.

It is your own fault!

In her bachelor's dissertation one of my students described the case of a woman (Özge), who in Bosnia had been raped by several men and had become pregnant. After the rape, she received no moral support from her family. "Her mother ignored her and sent her away because she did not want to know about the rape. Her father and brother yelled at Özge. Her father hit her in the face and left the room threatening that she would have to atone for it with her death". (Weber, 2018, p.35) Luckily for her, Özge found a way to leave her parental family. She found refuge and support from her aunt in Germany. After the birth of her child, she was looked after by social workers and psychologically in a mother and child facility.

Sex addiction

Addictive behaviours are characterised by:

- obsessiveness
- an ever-increasing tolerance threshold
- an escalation of dosage
- withdrawal symptoms
- carrying on despite negative consequences
- covering up the reality of the addiction
- complete loss of control

Sexual stimulation produces high levels of arousal, which is then accompanied by orgasm and sexual release, which are experienced as pleasurable. Therefore, because of the pleasure, it carries a high potential for addiction. Sex can work like a drug that is consumed initially just for the fun of it. However, as with any other drug (e.g. alcohol, nicotine, heroin or cocaine) when sex is practised too often, it loses its original power to satisfy, and there is a tendency to increase the dose of the drug and combine it with other drugs to try to attain the original effect. Therefore the desire for self-satisfaction becomes ever more intense, and the person looks for more and more extreme types of stimulation. He may frequently go to one prostitute and after a while to several. Three or four rather than two concurrent sexual relationships will seem to serve him better. He may be drunk, stoned and coked up as well. Adding pain and powerlessness into the mix by punishing or shackling can also be an attempt to enhance the sexual experience or at least bring it back to the level it was at the beginning.

The escalation of dosage and its accompanying excesses inevitably lead to more and more negative consequences (physical and psychological exhaustion, infections, spending large sums of money, the possibility of losing one's job etc.) and these must be accepted because otherwise withdrawal symptoms such as inner emptiness and anxiety threaten. Warning signals from the world around are skilfully pushed out of the way. The methods of fooling oneself and others are perfected, until at a certain point the entire edifice of lies collapses and comes tumbling down like a house of cards (Carnes, 1991, Melzer, 2018).

Sexuality and basic conflicts of interest

The principle of sexual reproduction does not make life easier and more peaceful for us human beings; instead it generates a number of serious conflicts of interest.

Conflict between self-preservation and procreation

When, as is the case with us humans, our offspring have to be nourished in the body of the mother for a long time, and after birth they need continuing intensive care, a lot of love and attention in order for them to develop into an independent individual, then the question for a woman is whether she wants to expend this enormous effort for the next generation at all. Can her body deal with these stresses and strains? What does she get in return? What does she have to give up for herself? Is it worth it for her to sacrifice her independence and professional career? Are the apparently innate instincts of her body to become pregnant and have a baby actually inescapable at a psychological level and do they have to be satisfied at any cost?

It also seems that there are many unconscious mechanisms at work that prevent women from becoming pregnant when they are not ready for it. First the unborn child has to persuade the maternal organism that it is not a foreign and hostile protein so it is not eradicated by the defence cells of her immune system (the phagocytes); spontaneous abortions and miscarriages are common occurrences amongst women. Since many human pregnancies originally are twin-pregnancies, the maternal organism is clearly very successful in preventing the further development of at least one of the children. If everything in the maternal organism is resistant to pregnancy, the newly developing child has to disguise himself very cleverly so that the maternal body mistakenly believes that the child is part of herself. By this means many children come into existence even when their mother does not willingly want it.

For men, who are supposed to take on paternal responsibility for the children, the question also arises under the patriarchal and competitive economic conditions: how much time and money is this going to cost me and what am I going to get out of it for myself?

There are animals that under stressful conditions eat their own young because the stress is too great. With us humans when parents are highly stressed, overwhelmed and impoverished the children are physically and psychologically at risk as well.

Throughout the world now contraception is a woman's business. The male contraceptive pill is not being developed at the moment because men are unwilling to put up with the associated side effects (Becker, 2017). They prefer to use a condom or, once the plan for a family has been completed, to have a vasectomy. For women, the most common and safe method, the contraceptive pill, puts their entire organism in a state of defence against fertilisation, which explains why many women complain of depression, headaches and inter-menstrual bleeding, and also about a decline in sexual desire (libido). The risks of long-term usage of 'the pill' depend on the particular preparation and combination of active ingredients contained in it, but in many cases may include deep vein thrombosis and embolism (Apotheken Umschau / The Pharmacy Magazine, 2019).

Abortions are also a massive violation of the female organism. Even in the best-case scenario, provided the woman has access to an experienced doctor, what appears on the outside to be a harmless surgical procedure or an uncomplicated taking of an abortion pill can still result in considerable psychological consequences. Aborting a pregnancy can represent a psychological trauma for the woman, which may significantly impair her future sex life and her partnership. By having an abortion a woman becomes the perpetrator against her own child, and in many cases, she traumatises herself in her psychosomatic identity, regardless of the mental reasons that have motivated her to execute the abortion (Hoppe, 2014). She would probably have to work on this psycho-trauma before becoming pregnant again so as to be emotionally open for her new child. In my practice I have seen this with numerous women, who carry within them this highly taboo topic of abortion as a part of their biography. Only when the psychological pain and confusion associated with the abortion are expressed can a fresh and unclouded joy for new life come into being.

Conflicts of interest between men and women

Many men lust after sex, whilst many women are frightened of sex and of being harassed. The #MeToo movement shows how widespread it is that men have the notion that they can unscrupulously turn their physical power and positions of influence to their sexual advantage, even in the liberal west. Societal structures based on dependency, lack of education and financial poverty make women vulnerable to blackmail and coercion for sex that they do not want.

Men idealise beautiful women and worship them as sexual goddesses. Sex idols like Marilyn Monroe or Romy Schneider were, as a consequence of their traumatic childhood experiences, anything but self-confident women. It was therefore not random that they ended up drug and alcohol dependent.

Some men will violently force a woman into sexual intercourse without her consent. When their sexual urges then are frustrated by the woman they desire, disappointment and rage quickly surface, which can be expressed in verbal abuse – 'whore', 'bitch' – or as manifest physical aggression. The spurned man may try to destroy the previously idolised 'dream woman' by any available means.

Because the weight of the work of reproduction in humans is unfairly distributed to the woman's detriment, women are often dissatisfied by how little they are supported by men in relation to it. Many men are not interested in the offspring that they have brought into the world; many do not even give financial support for the upkeep of their children. Many lose interest in the woman when she becomes pregnant, turning to another female who is not pregnant.

Some women also are not averse to extra-marital sex if they are ready to conceive and are in those moments unconcerned about hurting their partner, and may even be ready to foist someone else's child on their husband.

Conflicts within the sexes

Women compete for attractive men, and men may fight over a woman. The consequences of this are envy, jealousy and shame. Women and men sometimes try to oust troublesome rivals by any means available. It may even be that because of this intra-gender rivalry people find it difficult to think and act co-operatively at all. We think that we would be better off if we were positioned higher up in the gender hierarchy, but then overlook the unrelenting stress that this strategy puts on ourselves and others. So we isolate ourselves and become more and more lonely.

Conflicts between the interests of parents and children

Approximately one in every four pregnancies is deliberately terminated. Children who have survived an abortion attempt are not welcome afterwards either. Being a 'wanted child' is also not a guarantee for happy growth and flourishing either. Those children often find themselves under pressure to fulfil their parents' wishes and desires. For example, they should...

- take over the (family) farm or company;
- make their depressive parents happy;
- compensate for a dead sibling;
- become professionally what their mother or father did not manage to achieve;
- take care of their mother and become like a mother to her because she herself suffered from a lack of mothering;
- be the consoling and tender mother for the father that he did not have as a child.

From my psychotherapeutic practice I know that many children were not wanted, not loved and not adequately protected from violence or sexual abuse. Instead their traumatised parents had severely traumatised them.

Conflicts between siblings

Even though sibling love is a prevailing ideal and, although it may well exist, the reality often looks startlingly different, especially when the parents are traumatised. Siblings may have had to compete for the mother as a source of food. The shorter the gap between the two births, the harder it is for a mother to give both children the necessary attention. Siblings then experience each other as rivals for the mother's favour and possibly the father's support too. Even before birth, one twin may prevail at the expense of the other, so that the other dies before birth. Even when it comes to inheritances after the parent's death, the fighting and struggling between the parents often continue between the children.

Conflicts between different populations

A population of a species that successfully and rapidly proliferates will have to expand territorially. As a result, it becomes a threat to other populations of living creatures that inhabit a neighbouring territory. This also applies to human beings. We have multiplied so successfully across this earth that we are constantly displacing other populations of living beings from their habitats and causing the extinction of their species.

Since humans do not constitute a unified population, as distinct social units they are continually getting in each other's way. There are several possible ways in which such conflicts can arise:

- Hostile takeover of population A by population B: this we know from human history in the form of campaigns of conquest, colonialism, imperialism and capitalism. The defeated population is pushed aside, oppressed, impoverished and enslaved. This can even end up in genocide;
- Assimilation: Population A migrates into population B and to a great extent adopts the rules of live of population B. This is normally the case with labour migration, asylum

seekers and those displaced by war or migrating because of famine;
- Mixing: Population A and Population B mix or live side by side in a peaceful coexistence as long as no one points to their (for example religious) differences and tries to instrumentalize them for his power plays as was the case in the war in former Yugoslavia in 1990.

When different populations come into contact with each other, normally each one considers itself the best and really human. Religious, racist and nationalist ideologies are used to argue this case; that is why most populations are highly selective when it comes to their perception of reality, becoming trapped in their own patterns of group-thinking.

A population that is rapidly increasing sooner or later pushes for political, economic and ideological dominance within the territory in which it lives, causing many conflicts by this. If the population that has ruled up until this point then becomes a minority, it may take repressive measures against the rising population. This is likely to lead to a permanent conflict because populations increase more quickly when they are forced to live in poverty and misery, as is the case in the conflict between Israel and the Palestinians. The lack of education, material resources and willingness to practise effective contraception contribute to high rates of births. It has long been proven that the number of children a woman creates correlates to her level of education. When women are able to know more about themselves and their world, they are more likely to want to choose whether and when to bring children into existence. Frequently it is uneducated women who already have a child very young, aged fifteen or before, whereas the average childbearing age for female academics is nearly thirty. The time span between the generations has almost doubled here.

Competition or cooperation?

We do have a choice in our interpersonal relationships, as to whether to be competitive or cooperative.

- The orientation towards competition involves aggression, capitalistic ideas, colonialism, craving, cynicism, destructiveness, envy, fear, forging of alliances against others, greed, imperialism, intolerance, jealousy, lies, manipulation, need to win, obstruction of others, oppression, propaganda, racism, ruthlessness, self-superiority, spreading of ideologies, stress, striving for power, stupidity, war and so on ...
- Being cooperative means appreciation, collaboration, compassion, constructive criticism, desire for truth, finding compromises, joint efforts, love, openness, self-realisation, thoughtfulness ...

Babies and small children innately display cooperative behaviour. In a competitive environment however they quickly learn to be ruthless and selfish. Competition creates a fragile self-confidence (Kohn, 1989) and contaminates interpersonal relationships on every level:

- Between parents and children;
- Between men and women;
- Within the economy;
- Within politics.

In view of the serious conflicts of interest that can be associated with sexual reproduction no one should be allowed to be put under pressure or force themselves to have sex, or to become a parent. Sexuality is a creative potential that exists within every human being. However this potential should not be blindly and ruthlessly lived out in a destructive way, without regard for the consequences for partnerships, family structures and whole populations. Humanity will not die out if some men and women choose to remain childless or bring only a few children into the world. The current rate of increase in procreation, with the population already at 7.5 billion, will bring problems that we have not yet dreamt of.

How different societies would be when women can step forward with confidence and say "we will only give birth to children when we really want to, and when we are adequately supported emotionally and socially by our communities. As mothers, we want to be physically and emotionally present for our children long enough to ensure that they develop into healthy individuals. We are not willing to bring children into the world to end up toiling their lives away as labour slaves, or to serve as cannon fodder in war zones or to further increase the number of people with no perspective in their lives."

A clear inner decision is required to ensure that being a mother or a father is experienced as a personal benefit rather than a handicap. Those who, because of their own trauma, lack the ability to offer the child love, closeness and a clear 'I' as their reference point, should therefore make the effort to remedy these shortcomings through appropriate therapy. There may even be sufficient time during the pregnancy to do this. If not, it is not destiny or chance but a clearly predictable fact that the parents own psychotrauma-biography will be continued in their own children.

Becoming a parent and making it possible for your child to have a healthy development is not something that can be seen simply as a side-line issue for society. It is perhaps the single most important task of a society, so that living within one society and alongside different human populations can be shaped in the most constructive way rather than a destructive way. Traumatised children become traumatised adults, traumatised lovers and traumatised parents; they grow up into adult men and women who wreak havoc in society as a result of their trauma-survival strategies. What began for each individual in early childhood then ends in more and more traumatised and mutually traumatising societies on this globe (Ruppert 2019).

Sexual Psychotrauma

The human psyche

The human psyche is a data processing system that permeates the entire organism all the way down to a cellular level. Using pulsation, bodily fluids, nerve cells, organs and the brain as the central organ, this system comprehends reality both inside and outside the human organism in order that the individual person can survive and reproduce. Most of this is going on below the threshold of consciousness, with only a small fraction of all the information processed becoming a conscious reality for the individual human being. It is mainly with the help of our consciousness that we can voluntarily influence our reality and change it to suit our requirements. This also implies that there are some things that it is better for us not to influence too consciously but let it happen in its own unconscious way (e.g. birth processes).

The human psyche is a multimodal system. It includes perception (seeing, hearing, smelling, tasting, feeling), imagination, feelings, thinking, remembering, the intuitive understanding of relationships, being 'I', wanting and the ability to manage our own actions. These psychological functions are:

- Selective: specifically geared to each respective life situation and to our own interests and needs in the moment;
- Adaptive: able to adapt to different environments thereby making them our own;
- Creative: the ability to produce or invent something that has never existed before, and
- Reflexive: the human psyche can recognise itself and change itself because of what is perceived, felt and understood.

Although the human brain is a special organ capable of producing the highest performance on a conscious psychological level, the entire human body is capable of psychological insight. Each individual cell can absorb information via pulsations and fluctuations in the levels of chemicals. This is then processed, stored as a memory and the worked-through information can then be transmitted out to the external surroundings.

The basic functions of the psyche exist from the very beginning of a person's life, right after the union of the egg and sperm. For their development the child needs a supportive environment that allows their full potential to flower. In the earliest stages of life, prenatal, through birth and up to the age of three, the psychological functions of the child are easily vulnerable to disruption and can very quickly be overwhelmed. Therefore we can see that everything that happens in this early time has great importance for the future life of the person. Current pre-, peri- and postnatal psychology has accumulated a great deal of knowledge in this field (Evertz et al, 2014). Research shows that both unborn and newly born babies are extremely alert to what is happening to them and in their environment (Chamberlain, 1990).

What follows is a testimonial from a participant at one of my open-evening groups.

Feeling my mother's need already in the womb

"Towards the end of the time that my mother was pregnant with me, my parents were in a state of shock. As refugees they had been forcibly billeted in the spare rooms of a log-cottage after the end of the Second World War, and when another room became free my father had set up a shoe shop in it on credit. When the municipal administration found out about this, it threatened him with eviction because of misappropriation, if he did not immediately make the room available again as a living space. My parents hardly had enough money to buy anything to eat. This was the situation I was born into.

During a meditation under hypnosis, I was able to see that I was fully aware of this in the womb and wanted to express my love for my mother in order not to be an additional burden to her. I wanted to regress and stop being as a way of helping her. I came into the world as something dead and completely frozen. During this meditation I was very surprised at how strong a unit the mother and child is. It was as if we were one joint organism. My father had picked me up from the children's ward of the hospital without my mother's consent and dropped me off at a baby home. In that place I finally decided not to exist."

The human psyche can operate in three different states, which also influence our sexual life:

- State of well-being, in which we are most in touch with reality, because we do not feel existentially threatened. Well-being states are the primary basis for pleasurable experiences of sexuality.
- Stress states, in which an existential threat is experienced, which leads to a narrowing of the perception of reality. In such states the experience of pleasurable sexuality is not possible, instead it is coupled with fear, anger and aggression.
- Trauma states in which reality must be suppressed because it is impossible for the psyche to process it. Sexuality can then only be experienced and practised in a dissociated state.

A person's psychological identity is the sum of his life experiences from the very beginning. In order to be psychologically healthy, a person must be able to express and develop the following:

- his own 'I',
- his own want,
- his own perceptions,
- his own feelings,
- his own ideas,
- his own thoughts,
- his own words and his own language,
- his own actions.

We humans are social creatures. Our psyche is geared towards living together with other people, and with our psyche we can brilliantly understand and shape our relationships. I even suspect that we have a sense for this, the sense of relationship, which works in a similar way to our other senses of perception, i.e. seeing, hearing, smelling, etc. Our bonding sense of connection works immediately, spontaneously and without the need for detour via any higher cognitive functions, without thinking and talking.

Because of this unconscious connection there is a risk that a person may not be able to distinguish herself from another person, especially if she sympathises with this other person. But it is nevertheless essential that the psyche of each human is personal, that it belongs only to this particular person and has its point of reference in her own 'I'. If the psyche loses its personal quality, if the point of reference to the 'I' is lost, the entire psyche falls into a state where it is at the mercy of external influences. Without an 'I' of our own, the psyche can be captured so to speak by the psyche of another, for example by one's mother or father. Only an 'I'-centred psyche can create constructive relationships with other people in which everyone can remain himself or herself.

The human psyche is a result of the evolution of life, so it also has instinctive functions that secured the life and survival of our human and animal ancestors millions of years ago. It is an evolving and open system that is not genetically determined in terms of the ongoing necessary recognition of an always changing reality. Genes are only the potential, the accumulated knowledge of how life works in general. The psyche uses the pool of genes that can help it to cope with the respective realities of life.

The human psyche is enormously capable of learning. In a continuous development process the psyche can continually unfold its qualities as long as no traumatisations have taken place. Being human means becoming human. Every human being is a part of evolution and influences it in his own way. Traumatisation considerably restricts the development of human potentials, and can even set people back to pre-human stages of evolutionary development. Especially when the emotional comprehension of reality no longer functions, the cognitive assessments are no longer correct either. Without the help of our emotions we then do not recognise logical contradictions and become more and more entangled in our own web of thoughts, and increasingly confused and without orientation.

General characteristics of psychotrauma

Psychotraumas are the result of a person's experience when his psychological capacity to cope has been exceeded, and it has left him in a state of powerlessness and helplessness, at the mercy of others. One of the reasons for being overwhelmed can be that there is too much information for the psyche to process, for example during a car accident. The human psyche is traumatised more than anything else when what it experiences is inherently contradictory, and the person is forced to question his understanding of himself and the world (Fischer and Riedesser, 1998). So, when a child is beaten by his father whom he loves, he is unable to comprehend it. Is he my dear dad or is he a bad man? If the father also claims that he has to beat the child so that the child will grow up to be good, and that the beating is actually a service to him, then the confusion is complete for the child. Here the child's psyche can no longer fulfil its fundamental function of conveying reality to the child. What is true now? Being beaten hurts me? Or do I have to be beaten so that later I may grow up and then have to beat my own children?

In such situations, the human organism is first exposed to stress. He tries to eliminate or escape the perceived danger by attack or flight. So long as the affected person is still capable of physical reactions, the mobilised energy can be used and thereby defused. As soon as it is clear that this is not possible and only leads to more threats and pain (which is the normal situation for children in relation to their physically and psychologically superior parents), the emergency brakes are activated, and the organism switches into the trauma emergency mode. The organism had been so far functioning at full speed and must now slam on the brakes. This means that the body's movements freeze, and the body initially solidifies and then becomes completely limp (Huber, 2003; Levine, 1998). The person involved submits to the threat that can now no longer be averted, and therefore she is forced to submit to the overwhelming power. If the state of perception continues at full alertness, the feelings (fear, rage, disgust, shame) and sensations (heat, cold, pain) present in this traumatising situation are numbed by hormones and neurotransmitters designed for this purpose. In this way, the person does not feel her body, and therefore does not feel herself anymore. She experiences herself as in a cocoon beyond reach, but seemingly protected. A mental drifting off occurs; the current reality is no longer adequately and completely captured, but only seen in fragments, nebulous and hazy. The person concerned often can no longer consciously remember later what she has actually experienced. Overall, there is a splitting up of the coherent psychological structures. Perception, sensation, feeling, thinking, remembering and action do not work together anymore and begin to lead separate lives as parts of one and the same person.

Even if a person has survived a traumatising situation, either by chance or because a perpetrator has finally let him go, unfortunately these inner states of psychological fragmentation cannot dissolve, recover and reintegrate on their own accord. Rather, they remain permanently in the state of trauma, particularly when contact with the perpetrator continues and is unavoidable for the victim. This is particularly true for children who have to continue living with a parent who traumatises them. Since the split off unresolved trauma energies can be re-triggered at any time, there must be from this point on the establishment of a separate psychological mechanism that reacts immediately with countermeasures as soon as the trauma memories are reactivated. This means that the whole organism has to use a lot of energy to keep itself in check in order not to get out of control. Psychotraumas therefore lead to an internal splitting of the whole person. Their psychological and physical oneness is lost.

The relationship between body and mind becomes extremely weakened. In essence, traumatised human beings now exist in three different forms:

- as someone whose psyche can continue to grasp and comprehend reality as long as it is not confronted with sensations that trigger the psychotrauma;
- as someone who is still in a state of trauma in relation to a triggering situation, and
- as someone who tries to deny and repress the reality of his experience of powerlessness (see Figure 3).

Consequently, from this moment on being traumatised is part of one's identity and, at the same time, the reason why we cannot develop our originally healthy identity further. Experiences of psychotrauma are therefore not something that can be ignored and dismissed as trivialities.

From now on I can only really understand my life if I take into account the fact that I am traumatised, and others can only understand me if they know that I experience reality on three different levels and behave inconsistently as a result. I sometimes act from my healthy parts, but I also repeatedly enter states of retraumatisation or I find myself in a state of permanent stress and then my survival parts take over. Often, when I feel threatened, I immediately switch into the trauma emergency mechanism and into my survival strategies without the intermediate step of the stress reaction that would keep me dealing consciously with the actual situation. The more often this happens, the faster it happens. From now on, I am traumatised and divided within myself until I find a way to release my psychological fragmentation.

It is an unfortunate fact that because our psyche is in this traumatised state, we find it very difficult to distinguish between healthy psychological reactions and trauma survival strategies. The principle of survival strategies is not to admit the reality of one's own traumatisation. Therefore, we still pretend to ourselves that it is still possible to prevent the traumatisation that has

Love, Lust and Trauma

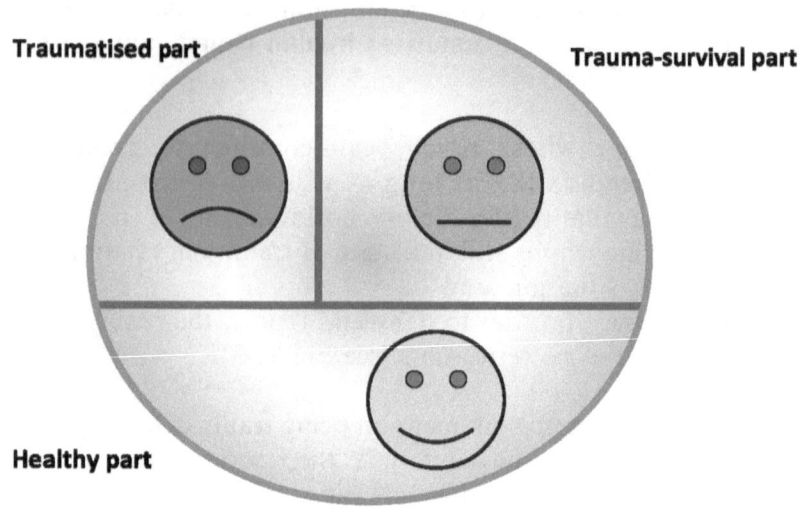

Figure 3: How a person splits after an experience of psychotrauma into three parts

already happened. A huge amount of time and life energy is spent protecting oneself from something that has actually happened. This has enormously harmful consequences for the life of each individual as well as for living together in communities. The illusion of being able to prevent something that has already happened paradoxically leads to further traumas.

- Split off from our feelings, we develop a pseudo-rationality with which everything can be justified as essential and inevitable (beating children, raping them, killing them, exporting armaments, throwing bombs).
- We normalise what is damaging and insane (prostitution and pornography).
- We cite others who think and do the same thing as us ('This is one of our cultural traditions!'), when in reality these things are not all right because they do serious damage to ourselves and others.

- We aggressively resist when someone challenges our delusionary creations, which we have developed as survival strategies.
- To conceal the cruelty of the reality that is created from our trauma-survival strategies, we use pseudo-scientific language and invent concepts to hide behind ('collateral damage' when innocent people are killed in a drone attack; 'mastectomy' when a woman, despite any physical necessity, has her breasts cut off).
- We discuss the pros and cons of inhumane behaviour, where there is actually nothing to discuss – inhumane behaviour is inhumane.
- We refer to supposed feelings and sensations where there are basically no real feelings at all. We may talk about feelings, but we do not feel.
- We live in an illusory world and do not notice that we are doing so.
- We always think that others are to blame.
- We moralise and judge instead of sticking to the facts. We confuse facts with judgements.
- We suck other people into the vortex of our trauma survival strategies with our confused thinking.

When we live in our trauma survival strategies, we seek external confirmation because we do not have a secure point of reference within ourselves. We want to be recognised by others and considered as normal and reasonable. A small cartoon (see figure 4), drawn by two seminar participants, expresses this succinctly. Those who offer 'comforting lies' are more in demand from traumatised people than those who tell 'unpleasant truths'.

Love, Lust and Trauma

Figure 4: What do I want? Comforting lies or unpleasant truths? (drawing by Benita Schmidt and Sarah Brüggesch)

Difficult feelings: anger, shame, pride and disgust.

Since anger, shame, pride and disgust are emotional qualities that are closely associated with sexuality, I would like to take a closer look at them. In my opinion, feelings can be analysed from three different angles:

- What are each of these feelings and what is their function?
- In which relational and social context do they arise?
- In which section of the splitting model that I have designed can they be found?

Anger

When we are rejected, attacked and hurt, anger is an appropriate emotional response. It can help us defend and protect ourselves. In trauma situations, however, anger does not help us because the perpetrator is stronger than we are, and the more we resist the more life-threatening the situation becomes. Therefore, the anger reaction must be suppressed and split off.

This repressed impotent rage then remains as a trauma feeling, and like all trauma feelings, it forms a background in our daily lives. We do not dare to express this rage to anyone stronger than us; however, people we consider weaker than ourselves are in danger of having our pent-up rage vented upon them. This is what children do when they act out their anger towards their parents on other children, for example their siblings, school mates or animals.

There is also a desire for revenge, directed towards the original perpetrator that continues to function unconsciously. Many women who have been raped would like, if they could, to cut off the penis of their abuser. This leads to a fixation on the original perpetrator, and then all men are placed under suspicion of being potential rapists. For many sexually traumatised women, even the smell of a man is hard to bear. Trauma victims easily become trauma perpetrators because of their anger and their desire for revenge. For example, a sexually traumatised woman can be triggered by contact with a man, and then react aggressively towards her young son.

Men often redirect the anger they feel towards their mother, which they cannot express, towards other women, so they may take very brutal revenge on those women they confuse with their mother. This can result in vicious rape, or even murder.

So far I have not seen that the expression of pent-up anger towards the perpetrators in a therapy session has led to any significant progress in healing. On the contrary, the inner splits may even deepen, because the traumatised child parts of us become afraid of these outbursts of anger. Therefore, such outbursts of rage are psychotrauma survival strategies for both victims and perpetrators, which only generate further stress, keep them entangled and create possibly even new psychotraumas. This will not lead to a way out of the perpetrator-victim dynamic.

Shame

When we feel ashamed, we are suffused with waves of heat, our heart races, our face flushes and our ears burn. Ideally we would like to hide, sink into the ground or disappear into thin air. We feel ashamed because we have done, or even only thought, something that goes against our own values and standards and those of other people who are important to us. We can also be ashamed because others who are important to us have embarrassed us or applied their own standards or values to us, for example thinking that we have physical defects, are not properly dressed, have lied or are stupid.

Young children usually have no sense of shame about their nudity and genitals. However they quickly sense if their mother or father thinks it is good or bad when they appear naked or play around with their genitals in their first phases of exploring their own body. Moral and religious commandments make a strong focus on sexuality and try to ensure that children behave morally and are 'chaste'.[9]

Shame is part of a healthy psyche because it reminds us that we have made a mistake or done something that is not appropriate for the community in which we live. What is important is whether the community is also living from a healthy psyche and is not making nonsensical rules. So, in most societies today no one will seriously disagree that sex with children is illegal. So anyone who engages in this has every reason to be intensely ashamed.

If the feelings of shame become so great that they cannot be integrated into the existing psychic structure, if the person cannot find a way to cope with the causes and triggers of his shame, then these feelings end up split off into the traumatised parts in my model of splitting. These feelings must be numbed, suppressed and locked away; there is no chance for them to be processed. This is why adults may still have child parts in them that feel like they will die of shame. All the feelings of shame that arise when we do something that our psyche cannot cope with, such as seriously hurting someone, or even murdering them, must be packed away.

One of the worst trauma feelings is the shame of existence, the shame of being alive at all, due to not being wanted by our parents, or of being in a certain social situation, for example a refugee who has had to flee to another country. There is nothing that one can do against this fundamental 'no' to ourselves from other people. It is not about anything that I do that is wrong, which could be corrected, but about my very existence itself. I am a problem because I exist and I am here, it does not matter what I do or fail to do.

Shame can also act as a trauma survival strategy. For example, we may feel shame when we go into a victim attitude in the hope of not provoking the perpetrator any further to reject us. This shameful attitude prevents us from clarifying the true causes of the shame; it is just a strategy of survival, and when we are in this survival part we are trapped in our shame, and submit completely to the perpetrator, identifying with him. We are afraid and cannot talk about the truth of what has actually been done and what often still continues to be done to us.

This also applies to perpetrators who have traumatised other people. When confronted with their acts of perpetration, they lower their heads, fall silent and cannot admit publicly what they have done. They even often manage to get others to let them off, because their feelings of shame then spread to the others and touch upon those people's own issues of shame. The whole thing often ends in awkward and embarrassed silence. This is one of the reasons why perpetrators of sexual trauma expect that people will not directly address their actions and confront them. They can rely on the shame of others; they will go on the offensive and shame others so that no one feels the impulse to accuse them of their actions. For example, if a mother realises that her husband is sexually traumatising her daughter, she will often remain silent because she is ashamed of what her husband is doing. Often the man goes on the offensive and accuses her of being a lousy wife and mother.

Pride

Pride has contrary sensations to shame; the body stands straight, the chest swells, the gaze is fixed straight ahead. Mothers and fathers will gladly declare themselves 'proud parents' in announcements of the birth of their child. We want to be seen and admired by other people for what we have achieved, or for how we physically present ourselves. So, pride is associated with particular achievements, or with how we style our bodies through plastic surgery, tattoos or body-building.

Pride means it is essential that others see us and recognise us. There may be good grounds to praise us, but there are also many strange reasons why people are awarded medals and decorations, or are highly esteemed: for killing in war; for dominating other people; for patriarchal leadership of a family, including even violence against women and children; for what I consider to be absurd top performances at world championships and Olympic Games. I also find it strange when men photograph their penis and proudly send these pictures to women via WhatsApp, or boast to their friends as to how many women they have slept with. Also a woman proudly presenting her bared breasts in public is from my point of view a questionable display. This belongs more in the area of psychotrauma survival strategies than in the healthy parts of the psyche.

The feeling of wounded pride can be so extreme that the only thing left to do in this moment is to split the feeling off and suppress it, where it leads a restless existence in the underground of our psyche. This can also result in a need for revenge as a trauma compensation strategy. We want to do the same to the person who has hurt us so badly, so that they also realise how painful it is. In the immediate trauma situation there is often a tremendous feeling of anger and intense hatred towards the perpetrator. There may even be a desire to kill them, but because we are in our trauma survival part we ignore the original reason, and the feeling only exists in our consciousness as a gnawing stress. So the need for revenge can then end up being directed against those people who are there in the present moment and within immediate reach rather than the original perpetrator. Usually these targets of our rage are completely innocent people who have done nothing to us, at least not the thing that caused us such hurt in the core of our existence. The true culprits then, as so very often happens, get off scot-free. Thus, many women who have been raped feel hatred and rejection towards all men, even if they were actually humiliated and degraded by only one man. It seems easier to feel the hate towards all men, than to deal with the specific perpetrator.

There can also be a healthy pride, and this can be a psychological resource for a person's life in the future; for instance if someone has dealt with the psychotraumas from their childhood to such an extent that it no longer impedes their present-day life. Then the person may have the courage to openly discuss and work on her sexual psychotrauma in a therapy group; this is often also very helpful for others with similar biographies and surely deserves our admiration.

Disgust

Disgust is a warning feeling so that we do not touch certain things, put them in our mouth, eat or drink them. It is also there to prevent us from letting certain things be done to us. Disgust reactions include nausea, feelings of gagging or vomiting. Disgust often occurs in relation to human body excretions: sweat, urine, faeces or bad breath. Vaginal fluids, menstrual blood and sperm can likewise trigger intense disgust reactions, especially when there were traumatizing experiences connected with it.

Such natural disgust reactions can, however, be misused to demonise the whole field of sexuality and construct an ideal in opposition to it of purity and cleanliness. Because then it can be claimed that the whole of sexuality is unclean and must be purified through rituals and regulations. Doctrines of genital circumcision, 'chastity' and 'virginity' are imposed on young women and men with fury and violence. When they have yielded to this authority, the survival parts of them must now believe that this is natural and that there is no alternative. The victims then make a tradition out of it, and continue to exercise the same violence against their own daughters and sons.

Disgust feelings are more immediate than shame feelings, because they are less easily influenced by the mind and are directly connected with smell or taste sensations. When something smells foul, it is difficult for others to convince us that it is actually delicious. However, smell and taste sensations are also dependent on habits and can be influenced and passed on at an early age, sometimes even prenatally. Epigenetic research in mice, for example, found that when the smell of cherry blossom is coupled with electric shock, that smell can still trigger trauma reactions in the grandchildren's generation (Spiegel-Online 2013).

Anyone who is forced to ignore their feelings of disgust and is persuaded to do something he or she does not like (e.g. acting out oral sex) has to split these feelings off. These feelings can then be triggered on inappropriate occasions. For example, if the taste of sperm engenders disgust in us, we might be at a dinner party and suddenly feel like throwing up because the food we have been offered reminds us of sperm.

For this reason, we must always ask whether the disgust we are currently feeling actually has something to do with the present situation or whether it is the result of a trauma memory. As long as we are in our trauma survival parts, we will deny that and prefer to look for a reason in the present, so that we do not have to deal with our past: "I was sexually abused? I really can't imagine that is true!" We would rather take a tablet for our headaches and nausea, drink alcohol or a stomach-soothing chamomile tea than face the truth that our experience of disgust is pointing to.

The Psychotrauma Biography

The attempt to describe psychotraumas and their consequences in a general form, and to reduce them down to an overall concept, requires concretisation, since there are different occasions and causes for psychotraumas. My first attempts to distinguish between psychotraumas led to the following classification (Ruppert, 2011):

- Existential Trauma: a matter of life and death – the fear of death has to be split off, feelings of extreme panic have to be suppressed (e.g. through drugs, medication, breathing them away).
- Trauma of Loss: The loss of a loved one creates unbearable grief, the pain of loss must be suppressed, the lost person is kept psychologically present and alive in our fantasies.
- Bonding Trauma: When a mother does not succeed in bonding with her child, the child must suppress the pain of rejection and loneliness; the illusory hope of motherly love remains for the rest of his life.
- Bonding System Trauma: abuse, incest or murder in the family system lead to unbearable feelings of guilt and shame in both the victims and the perpetrators, which have to be split off; on the outside a façade of a healthy world is built up.

Based on years of psychotherapeutic experience with traumatised people worldwide, and the intermediate step of including traumas that happen prenatally, during birth and immediately after birth into my thinking (Ruppert, 2016), I have come to the following classification of psychotraumas. This is more focused towards the course of a person's life and assumes that there is a logical sequence of psychological trauma (see Figure 5). It is no longer a question of looking at isolated psychotraumas, but a whole life can be lived under the influence of psychotrauma from the outset.

Psychotraumas that arise because of natural disasters are left out of this model, although they can also be traumatising in terms of existential trauma and trauma of loss, and will presumably affect more and more people in times of climate change, even in previously temperate climate zones.

In the following section, I set about defining and describing the trauma of identity, the trauma of love and the trauma of being a perpetrator oneself, and thus explaining the contexts in which the trauma of sexuality is embedded.

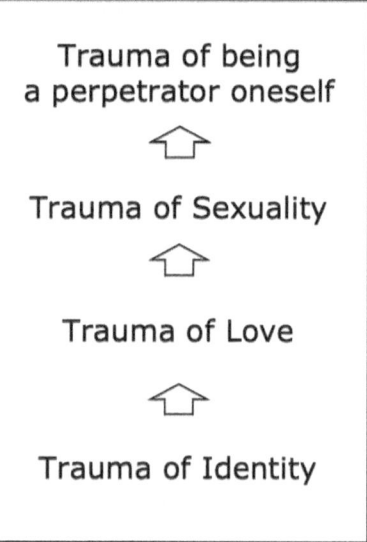

Figure 5: The Psychotrauma Biography

The Trauma of Identity

It is a contradiction for a woman to get pregnant and have a child grow in her belly and for her not to want to bring that child into the world. Such a situation is physically and psychologically unbearable for the mother, and is also catastrophic for the child, because at the beginning of his life he is utterly reliant on his mother and is in desperate need of her love and kindness. The primary trauma, or so to speak the 'mother of all human traumas', is therefore the 'trauma of identity': my mother rejects me and does not want me. I am not supposed to exist! I should not be here! I am a burden and an obstacle for her and her future life.

It is therefore also quite likely that the pregnant woman will attempt an abortion in order to get rid of the unwanted child, if her unconscious immune responses do not manage this on their own. If a child survives an abortion attempt, he already suffers an existentially threatening situation while in the womb.

The most important thing about identity trauma is that already the unborn child must split off his own unconditional 'yes' to his own existence and his own love for himself, and therefore loses his connection with himself. He must betray and abandon himself.

His survival strategy is then to adapt as best he can to his mother's 'no'. He has to suppress his zest for life and his confidence in living, and he has to give up his own 'I' and his own 'want' in order to make himself as inconspicuous as possible and subordinate himself to his mother's needs and ways of thinking (see Figure 6).

Through this act of self-abandonment, the child ends up in a state of fundamental dependence on his mother, which he would never feel had he not been traumatised in this way. Because he has had to give up his own 'I', he is no longer living from his own self and out of his own power. He then experiences himself as utterly dependent for his survival on the relationship with his mother and everything that is external to himself.

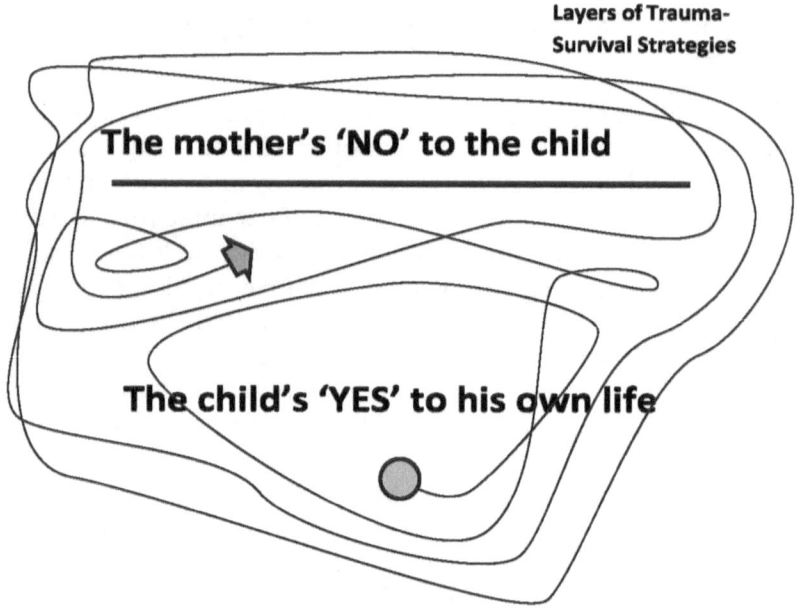

Figure 6: The Trauma of Identity as the lifelong struggle to adopt our mother's 'NO' as our own.

To compound things further, a pregnant woman herself may not want to live. There may be a part of her that feels a pull towards death. Perhaps she would ideally like to kill herself. It is not uncommon for women who did not wish to get pregnant to think not only of an abortion but also of suicide. The child feels this whilst he is still in her belly and so from the beginning gets mixed up in this pull towards death that belongs to his mother.

He must then spend a lifetime fighting against this undercurrent in his psyche whenever it rears up, so that he does not hurl himself off into death. What may appear from the outside to be a completely incomprehensible lifelong suicidal tendency often has its roots in a mother's wish to die.

On a basic level, the dark clouds of the mother's traumas energetically float above the child who, once implanted in her uterus, is directly connected via the umbilical cord to all the

The Trauma of Identity

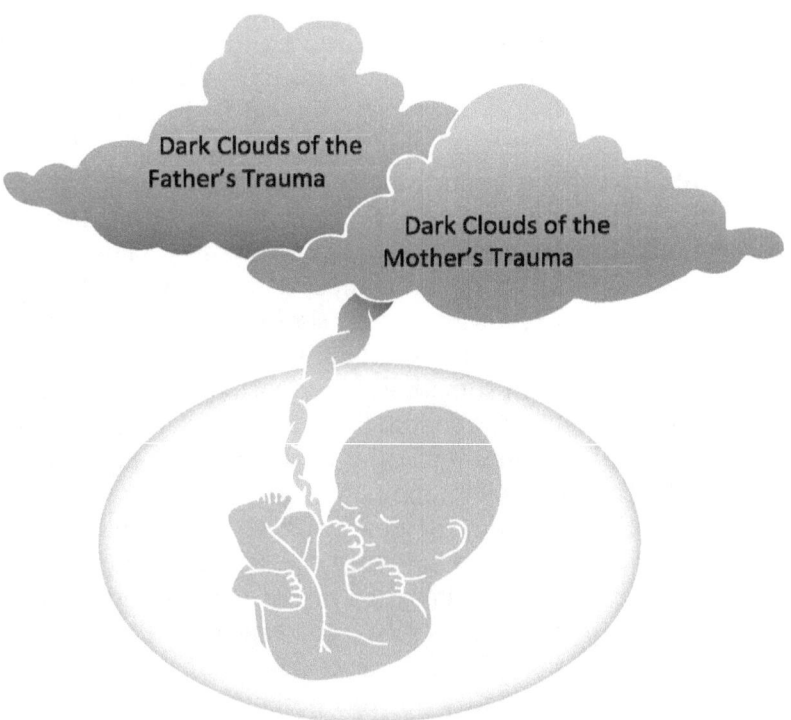

Figure 7: The child already experiences in the womb the dark clouds of maternal and paternal psychotraumas.

hormonal consequences these traumas have. As well the father's traumas can have an effect on the unborn child from outside (see Figure 7).

In the therapeutic work, this traumatisation from before birth often appears as a battlefield on which the individual psychological parts of the yet unborn child lie around like wounded soldiers, frozen in shock. As a result, the birth process itself is even more traumatising, because on the one hand the mother is not active enough during the labour to bring the unwanted child into the world, and on the other hand, the child is also lacking the desire and joy to be born. Usually there is only one survival part that desperately wants to get out of the mother's womb, as this will end the intra-uterine suffering. Many other parts remain split-off in the womb, or get stuck in the moment of the birth process. This trauma dynamic, coupled with a medical system that is technology-fixated and obsessed with maximising profits (Emerson, 2017; Mundlos, 2015), is a fundamental reason why so many birth processes involve acts of violence towards the mother and the child, including forceps delivery, vacuum extraction or caesarean sections (WDR, 2019).

A variation of the trauma of identity is when a woman wants a child as a trauma-survival strategy, in order to avoid contact with her own psychotrauma. Through this long yearned 'wanted' child, such women (and sometimes their partners too) hope that they themselves will be freed from their own fears and feelings of hopelessness and loneliness. The child is supposed to give them a purpose in life that they do not otherwise have. The child is required to help a woman; for example, to bind her man to her or to prevent him from leaving when the relationship goes into crisis. 'Wanted' children like this are not there for their own sake; instead they must fulfil a purpose for their mother or father (for example: to become the male successor in a family business). Such children are just an idea for their parents. But children have real physical needs; they show feelings, they want physical contact, they cannot control their excretion, they become ill; they develop angry feelings towards their parents if they are not sufficiently physically cared for and loved. Through the reality of pregnancy, birth and the natural exuberance of the child, mothers are, in many ways, at risk of coming into contact with their trauma feelings and tend to escape into their mind to protect themselves from these. As a result they split even further from their feelings and from their bodies, and so suppress the child's expressions of life in order not to endanger their inner stability. In the absence of their own proper feelings, they try to feel through their children.

Such ideas of being a wanted child force us to deny our own needs and feelings from the outset and to keep in check our exuberance for life in order to satisfy the expectations of our parents, and not to endanger their psychological stability. Only

The Trauma of Identity

if we serve their survival strategy do we have a right to exist. When we begin to develop our own ideas and needs, we are skilfully manipulated by our parents' survival strategies to give them up: "You don't want to make your mother sad, do you?" "It's going to be your fault if your mum gets upset and becomes ill!" The children then start to take on the split-off trauma energies of their parents and soak them up like a sponge. The child becomes a container for his parents' trauma feelings.

This process begins in the womb; the children also try to protect themselves from this emotional appropriation by the parents, while at the same time, some parts of themselves withdraw into a shell as best they can.

The main survival strategies in a trauma of identity are:

- escape into identification (e.g. escaping into the role of mother, spouse or profession)
- hiding behind a 'we' ("We are a perfect family!")
- defining oneselves by a sexual role ("I'm a real man!", "I'm a transvestite.").

Because an understanding of the trauma of identity is vital in understanding the psychological core of ourselves and other people, here is a summary of the underlying logic of this form of trauma:

1. I emerge from the fusion between two primal life forces, an egg and a sperm cell. This is my starting point of my life energy, my will to live and my joy in life. My golden essence so to speak. I am and I want to be. There is not the slightest doubt about that in myself.
2. In the womb I feel a threat from outside, the rejection of my existence or a complete lack of interest in me. This is caused by my mother and what influences her; for example the unwillingness of my father, who does not want me to be his child.
3. In the long run I cannot withstand the forces of such rejection and being ignored. In this emergency situation, I

split off from myself because I cannot deal with it in any other way. A part of me remains back in the womb, preserved in this traumatised state of being a child who is not wanted. The other part of me switches sides, and after birth I try to ally myself with the perpetrator (my mother) or both perpetrators (my mother and father). I identify myself with their rejection of me. I hide my own 'I' away and adopt a victim attitude. With my survival 'I', I serve my parents: "I will do everything you expect from me so that I may survive and be allowed to be here. I will make myself as inconspicuous as possible so that I will not be a burden to you."

4. In the course of this process, my own 'I' and myself become strangers to each other and what actually belongs to the real stranger, the psyche of my mother and father, I experience as my own.

5. It is necessary for my survival 'I' that I no longer recognise the fact that the original source of rejection comes from my parents. I now experience them as the 'good guys' who give me support and orientation and without whom I would be nothing.

6. Therefore I no longer associate the threat with my mother and/or father but rather with something else that exists outside of the relationship with 'my parents'. Somewhere out there, there is something 'evil' that is threatening.

7. But this threatening and 'evil' thing is buried in my own psyche because it stems from my split-off life essence. I now experience my original golden essence with all its vitality as the most threatening thing imaginable. Simply wanting to be me and be here, I now consider as something impossible and selfish.

8. The survival part of me that has identified with 'my mother' and 'my father' sooner or later starts to feel their weaknesses and their demands. So I make myself available to them by giving them my life energy. I feel my original perpetrators, who I have psychologically transformed into my benefactors, are suffering. And so it now becomes my

life's task to keep 'my benefactors' alive and to protect them from attacks from other people, possibly until the end of their lives.
9. As my life goes on, I will no longer search for the 'gold' inside myself but will look for it externally: in the beautiful gleam of money, wealth and the admiration of others.
10. Now I know that I can only get this admiration if everything I do is presented as in service to others and for the good of a higher purpose. Because those others around me have also internalised early on that simply being myself is an immoral arrogance.

When we understand this logic we can also understand why people become narcissists, psychopaths, patriots and nationalists; why they are afraid of 'strangers' and why they see them as fundamentally unpredictable and 'evil'. It is then clear why they become aggressive and attack completely innocent people – it is because of the unconscious prenatal fear of death. Xenophobia is also the consequence of the self-rejection that often turns into self-hatred in the course of identity trauma. This then also blocks self-love and the knowledge of what good self-care might look like.

As dangerous as Donald Trump is at present, because as President of the USA he always has with him the briefcase with the launch codes to deploy the nuclear missiles, his prominent example could help us all to learn more about the trauma of identity and its consequences.

Trump's wall

Why, for example, does the powerful president of the United States of America, Donald Trump, desperately need a wall to ward off the 'tide' of 'evil' people who want to come to 'his' country? What did he experience in his mother's womb as 'evil'? Only he could find out for himself if he had the courage to do so. His schizophrenic upbringing has been well documented: on the one hand he was belittled by his father time and time again whilst at the same time spurred on by him not to submit to anyone (D'Antonio, 2016). He is a typical victim of an age-old pattern: the father sees in his son a male rival whom he has to keep down. The son is not allowed to become bigger than his father. Some sons then do not try this at all. This was probably the case with Trump's older brother Fred, who died at the age of 40 because of alcohol consumption. Others, however, like Donald Trump, take up the challenge with their father. This then ends up in a relentless competition, which can only end in the self-destruction of the son. The son will always lose emotionally in this test of strength, no matter how many successes he may lay at the father's feet. Since the son is in reality looking for the love and recognition of his father, it is easy for the father to devalue all the 'gold' the son shows him, and to claim that it is just worthless tinplate. Donald Trump treated his own son, Donald Trump Jr. the same, as his father, Fred Sr., treated him. Following the logic of identity trauma 'My right to exist means making myself useful to the perpetrator'. Donald Jr. now also worships his father, despite all the humiliations he has had to take from him. He increasingly supports him with aggressive speeches against his political opponents (Tagesanzeiger newspaper, 2018).

Among the stars of the film, music and sports industry there is enough illustrative material to study identity traumas and their manifold consequences. Here is an example of a football star:

My golden calf

Against the background of identity trauma, the urgent need that stars from the entertainment industry have to be admired and bathe in the golden glow of the media spotlight becomes understandable. In this way we can also understand their disappointment and anger when they are not granted this idolatry. This happened, for example, to an ex-football star of Bayern Munich. He celebrated his desire to be someone very special by ordering a steak in a restaurant that was wrapped in gold leaf that cost him 1200 euros. He put a video of it on Instagram. When a *wave of criticism rebounded at him for it, he struck back savagely: "I am constantly criticised by these pseudo-journalists for my actions (the most recent example: the price of my food!)". But, he goes on, if he does good, it is not acknowledged: "Why don't the mass media report about that? They prefer instead to talk about the holidays I spend with my family. They scrutinise my actions and what I eat. They have the time for all that kind of nonsense!" Then the 35-year-old really let off steam. "To the envious, angry people who are only in the world because of a perforated condom: F**k your mothers, your grandmothers and your whole family tree," writes Ribéry. His success, he claims, is based only on him and those close to him who believed in him. All the others are just little stones in his shoes, the Frenchman continues. (Abendzeitung newspaper, 2019)*

Those who are rejected or perhaps even hated normally do better if they do not relate these negative feelings to themselves, but to leave those feelings with the people who reject and hate them. If they can do this there is clarity as to who is the victim of these attacks and who is the perpetrator. However, the trauma of identity, split off into the unconscious, creates fundamental confusion amongst many people. The victims become perpetrators against themselves. They love their perpetrators and hate themselves. In this way, the victim-perpetrator dynamic created in early childhood is carried out into society. Because perpetrator-victim dynamics are so widespread in the world, we can see this as evidence of how many children on this earth suffer from being unwanted or, as 'wanted' children, who are supposed to compensate for their parents' traumas.

The Trauma of Love

If a child is rejected by his mother in himself, and has to split off from himself, he inevitably ends up in the next trauma dynamic, the 'trauma of love'. Denying the truth that his mother or father do not want him, the child continually strives for love and contact with his mother. He is constantly wondering how he must be to get her attention. He is at his mother's service, despite her ongoing rejection. Although he sometimes withdraws in disappointment, he is in no position to exist without contact with his mother.

If he were connected to himself, the unbearable feelings that he has split off because of the trauma of identity and his own inevitable self-betrayal would surface. Because the connection with himself is missing, he takes refuge in an identification with his mother. Without any relationship to her, the child feels as though he is nothing. The paradoxical formula for identity in the trauma of love is: 'I am what I *lack*, what I *don't* have and I *miss* – my mother's love'. The original, instinctive childlike love that the child has for the mother, then cannot develop into a more mature form of love. Love is then connected with feelings of dependency.

Even if someone is angry with his mother or hates her, it does not mean that he will abandon his relationship with her. On the contrary anger and hatred strengthen the fixation on having a relationship with her. This is based on the hope that the mother will finally see and acknowledge the child's own need, which is hidden behind the anger and hatred. One day she will wake up and love him. As long as the child has no opportunity to correct this illusion, he lives his whole life hoping that his affection and love, or defiance and rebellion, can melt the barbed wire of maternal and paternal trauma survival strategies (see Figure 8).

The Trauma of Love

Figure 8: The trauma of love and the child's tireless efforts to overcome the 'barbed wire' of his parents' survival strategies.

In relation to his mother, such a person always lives a shadowy existence. The mother is the focus and has the reins firmly in her hand. If necessary, she, who is herself traumatised, pulls out all her tricks and blackmails the child if the child wants something of his own, shows his own feelings or is no longer at her service. Some mothers (such as my own) even threaten the child with suicide if he is not there for her and will not do what she asks. This is because such a mother also does not have her own 'I' and her own 'want' at her disposal, and she is split off from her feelings and body. Therefore, as her survival strategy for her trauma of Identity, she abuses the child in many ways. Sons are then brought up as substitute partners and told that they must not abandon their mother under any circumstances. The mother often belittles the son's potential partners; she acts with jealousy against them.

As they go through their lives, those who are stuck in the trauma of love always need a relationship with someone, no matter how bad and full of conflict this relationship is. Being alone raises the danger that the original trauma feelings of pain, despair and loneliness will surface, which they will not be able to withstand.

Beyond the mother the next person for the emotionally dependent child, if he is there, is the father. If the child sees only the slightest chance, he tries to make up for the lack of mothering through connection with the father. Later in life it is the sexual partners or one's own children who are supposed to replace the person's lack of mothering. However, none of this will work. All it does is create similar relationships in later life, which are equally full of endless conflict. The person who is psychologically stuck in the trauma of love quickly assumes responsibility for others (parents, partners, their children) in order not to feel their own loneliness and abandonment. He deals with the problems and pain of others so as not to feel his own pain. This leads to complete overload and exhaustion and sooner or later to an inner state often called 'burnout'.

In addition, loss traumas (e.g. early death of the mother, or loss of own children) can have an effect on these already complex inner events and further complicate the person's inner dynamics. Here is example from the show business world.

Mr Schlemmer

The biography of the German comedian Hans-Peter 'Hape' Kerkeling is an example of the combination of an identity trauma with a loss trauma. He grew up with a depressed mother (born in 1930). All he knows is that after two miscarriages he was not planned and that his mother would have preferred a daughter rather than a son. In the year finally ending with her suicide, he desperately tried to cheer her up with his vivaciousness and wit. When he was eight years old, she took an overdose of sleeping pills in his presence. He directly witnessed her dying and blamed himself for not having saved her. His career as a comedian was deeply influenced by this. He could only split off the painful loss of his mother into his unconscious, but not overcome it. He also did what often happens as a consequence of an identity trauma: he identified himself with many other people. He skilfully imitated them and then invented new made-up characters with which he was identified by others (e.g. the famous figure of 'Horst Schlemmer'). His autobiography about his childhood is an impressive document of how a trauma of loss in its many facets is experienced by a child (Kerkeling, 2014).

Not being able to be with oneself because of trauma has many consequences. Notable symptoms for the trauma of love are:

- clinging,
- anxiety,
- neediness,
- attention seeking,
- not being able to be alone,
- constantly being busy,
- overly concerned about others,
- trying to dominate other people's lives.

Those who are trapped in a trauma of love feel worthless and ashamed of their own existence. Instead of simply being, they always have to judge everything and feel themselves being judged by everything. They search for purpose and meaning in the outside world because they have given up contact with their inner world from very early on.

The main survival strategies for the trauma of love are:

- immersion in illusions of love ("I know that my mother/my husband really loves me deep down despite everything"),
- creating love illusions about others ("You are my sunshine!"),
- seeing love as a miracle cure ("Love will heal all wounds."),
- sacrificing oneself for others because all efforts to be loved were always disappointed.

The following is an example of a man stuck in the trauma of love. He is a son of Dr Hans Frank, one of the main perpetrators of German fascism during the 2nd World War.

The Scarecrow

Dr Hans Frank (1900-1946) was an early supporter of Adolf Hitler, and from 1939 to 1945 he was Governor General in Poland, which the German fascists had conquered at the beginning of the war. There he was responsible for the cruellest of crimes committed against the Polish population. After the end of the Second World War he was hanged as one of the main war criminals by the Americans on the 16th October 1946. His son Niklas, born in 1939, and who his father believed was not conceived by him, in the year 2018 still carries pictures of his father in his breast pocket. He has spent much of his life researching his father's biography until his father's final minutes on death row in Nuremberg Prison. 'In the spring of 1968, he hammered out his rage into the typewriter. For four weeks he settled accounts with his father ... writing sentences like: "The cracking of your neck saved me a messed-up life." He described how as a child every year on the night of 16 October he would imagine his father's execution, and masturbate. In the summer of 1987 'Der Vater: Eine Abrechnung' ('The Father: A Reckoning'), was published (translated into English as 'In the Shadow of the Reich' (1991).' (Süddeutsche Zeitung, 2019a)

But his father, internalised by his trauma of identity and trauma of love, will not let go of him. Therefore, Niklas still acts out his trauma of love today – he hangs one of his father's coats on a pitchfork and exhibits it in his garden as a scarecrow. The illusion of a possible good father lives on in him: "As a lawyer my father could have fed the family very well in the Third Reich. He could have presented medical certificates to Hitler and the Party saying that unfortunately he could not continue to work in a leading position." (Süddeutsche Zeitung, 2019a)

Whole political movements can be seen as the expression of the trauma of love out of the trauma of identity. All their love is projected on 'the People' and ' the Fatherland'.

"We are the People!"

The trauma of love is also one of the psychological foundations of xenophobia, which is currently manifesting throughout Europe, producing populist parties and politicians. Citizens, out of their disappointed childlike psyche, see their leading politicians as their mum and dad, towards whom, as children, they were always well-behaved, loyal and obedient. They now become suspicious and rebellious when mum and dad let other children come into their country, take them into care (asylum) or even want to adopt them (give them citizenship). They experience this as unfair and feel forgotten. They want parents who see only them as legitimate, because they are their 'blood-related' children. Hence their cry "We are the People!" The terror that these advocates of an ethnically pure national community will exert against their own people the moment they are in power is predictable.

The trauma of being a perpetrator oneself

Before I continue to explain more about the trauma of sexuality in the next section, here are a few notes on what I call the 'trauma of being a perpetrator oneself'. In my experience, people only become trauma perpetrators because they are already victims of trauma. The 'trauma of being a perpetrator myself' is in this respect a separate trauma category, because a trauma perpetrator not only traumatises his victim, but also traumatises himself through his perpetrator actions. Since a trauma perpetrator still has healthy psychological parts that can perceive, feel and understand reality as it really is, feelings of guilt, shame and disgust about what he has done come up in him. As a result, he has to split off these unbearable feelings and he has to construct perpetrator attitudes as a trauma survival strategy. These attitudes should not only convince others, but also himself, that he is completely innocent and has not done anything bad.

Because of a perpetrator's own traumatisation, their healthy 'I' and their own 'want' have barely had a chance to appear during their life. Consequently they act from their survival 'I' structures and a 'want' that is programmed just to keep going. In these states they are cut off from their own healthy feelings and especially from feelings of compassion for themselves and for others. In this state they can do things a person acting from his healthy psyche would never do. Trauma perpetrators take no responsibility for what they do. In their perpetrator attitudes, they experience themselves as victims when they traumatise others, and may even see themselves doing right when they murder and rape. Because their perpetrator attitude wants to keep the fact of their perpetration hidden and not admit to what they have done, their acts of perpetration increase and become more frequent, until finally the perpetrator gets used to traumatising other people with a guilt-free conscience.

The full extent of psychotrauma biographies, which are currently lived in large numbers in Germany, are repeatedly brought to my attention either by social work students at the university where I teach, or through letters people write to me. Here is an example that shows how a victim of trauma who was not wanted, not loved and also not protected from sexual traumatisation as a child, may grow up to become an adult woman who constantly re-enacts sexually traumatising situations in her relationships with partners. Despite medical and psychological treatment, she pushes her trauma survival strategies to extremes, and finally, as a mother, becomes a perpetrator towards her own children. She was born in a viper's nest of a family, and has become equally venomous herself to her own children.

The psychotrauma biography of Mrs A.

Mrs A. had been forced to witness a lot of domestic violence in the early years of her life. Several times she had to watch her father severely abuse her mother, coercing her into prostitution. Mrs A. was three years old when her mother died of a sexually transmitted disease. Her father was in prison at that time and Mrs A. had to stay in the apartment with her dead mother for three days before she was rescued by the police.

The Trauma of Love

After her mother's death, she was placed in a home for several years. At the age of six her paternal grandparents took her into their house. When her father was released from prison and returned to his parents' home, he inflicted severe violence on Mrs A. and made her available to other men for sex. During this time she developed anorexia and bulimia, and because of these symptoms she was in and out of psychiatric treatment.

Ms. A. completed her education and married for the first time at the age of twenty. She lived with her husband at her grandparents' house for a few months before moving to another town. Her first son was then born. During her pregnancy she again suffered from eating disorders, and put on 60 kg in weight. The threat of pre-eclampsia was averted by hospitalisation during the pregnancy, and the child was born on the due date without complications.

Four months after the birth of her child, Mrs A. returned to work, so the boy spent a lot of time with his father's parents. There were always violent arguments between Mrs A. and her husband, since she felt dictated to by her parents-in-law with regard to bringing up her son. She did not feel sufficiently understood and supported by her husband. She again developed severe eating disorders and was hospitalised for six weeks. During this time she decided to separate from her husband, and subsequently divorced him.

Together with her son, she found a new home on a farm, and at the age of 30 she married the owner. One year later her second son was born. The marriage with this much older man was full of physical and psychological violence. Her husband drank a lot and cheated on her with three other women. These relationships resulted in several children. At times one of these women and her daughter also lived with them on the farm. After two years of suffering, Mrs A. got divorced and fled to a women's shelter. Two years later, however, she married this man again. Two years after that she once more found refuge in a women's shelter. She is currently in psychiatric treatment again.

Mrs A.'s older son is already known to the child protection services. He has great problems coping with life on his own and has repeatedly shown suicidal behaviour. The younger son from early on did not develop age-appropriately, and suffers repeatedly from seizures.

The Trauma of Sexuality

What is sexual psychotrauma?

A sexual psychotrauma is suffered when a person's body is used as the object for satisfying another person's sexual needs. He is thereby physically and psychologically injured without being able to resist or escape from the situation. This results in overwhelming feelings of pain, fear, grief, anger, disgust, shame, guilt and worthlessness.

I prefer to speak of sexual traumatisation rather than sexual 'abuse'. The word 'ab-use' is misleading because it implies that there could be a legitimate sexual 'use' of another person. It therefore seems important to me to pay attention to the phenomenon of psychological splitting that such experiences induce in a person: in particular the far-reaching loss of our healthy 'I', our grip on reality, and the serious consequences that these can have for ourselves, as well as for our fellow human beings.

The concept of psychotrauma also makes it easier to understand the motivations of the perpetrators. Instead of calling them 'sex monsters' or 'paedophiles ', it becomes clear that they are acting out of their trauma survival strategies; that they were trauma victims before they became trauma perpetrators, and that they continue to traumatise themselves with their acts of perpetration, and will continue to do so until they look at their own psychotrauma biography.

Although I speak of 'sexual violence' or 'sexual assault' in some parts of this book, I always mean the psychological dynamics of sexual traumatisation.

The forms that sexual psychotrauma can take vary:

- There may be sexual traumatisation during childhood with different degrees of severity.
- Rape of adolescents and/or adults taking place both within and outside of partner relationships.

- The transgression of sexual boundaries takes place in situations of economic dependency.
- Mass rape is a strategy of war; sexualised violence against women is used to humiliate the 'enemies', who are blamed for being unable to protect them. During and after wars the male penis sometimes becomes a deadly weapon.
- Child pornography, sexual torture and 'ritual abuse' are in many ways systematically practised (Huber, 2013; Nick et al., 2018).

In addition to these obvious sexual traumatisations, I also include:

- Male and female genital circumcision,
- Psychotraumas inflicted by the medical system on pregnant women and women giving birth (Mundlos, 2015; Witteck, 2019),
- Adult pornography and prostitution.

The German book 'Sexualität und Trauma' by Melanie Büttner (2018) provides a good overview of issues relating to the frequency of sexual trauma in women and men of different ages.

Secondary symptoms of sexual traumatisation

As with all types of trauma, sexual psychotrauma shows up by the symptoms that result because of it. Although they vary depending on the type and severity of the trauma, there are a number of phenomena that may be identified as physical and psychological signs of sexual trauma:

- fears that cannot otherwise be explained (for example: not being able to turn off the light when in bed at night),
- problems falling asleep because of symptoms such as headaches,
- an inability to sleep through the night and experiencing of night terrors,

- nightmares of evil monsters,
- wetting the bed or defecation during sleep,
- hypersensitivity to touch,
- eczema around the mouth,
- inflammation in the genital and anal area,
- bladder infections,
- pain when emptying the bladder or bowels,
- constipation and diarrhoea,
- inflammation of the gums,
- bad breath,
- grinding the teeth (bruxism) and whistling in the ears (tinnitus),
- sore throat,
- tonsillitis,
- shallow breathing, shortness of breath,
- back, hip and leg pain,
- strong muscle tension in the pelvic area,
- intense pain during sexual intercourse,
- vaginal cramps,
- dissociation during sexual intercourse or orgasm,
- disgust about sexual issues,
- impotence,
- numbness below the line of the navel,
- disgust with food that reminds us of sperm and mucus,
- compulsive cleaning and washing,
- heavy consumption of nicotine and alcohol,
- high consumption of sedatives, sleeping pills, laxatives,
- use of illegal drugs such as cannabis, heroin and cocaine,
- chronic depression,
- problems with concentration at school or at work,
- memory lapses and memory disorders,
- extreme attachment,
- extreme withdrawal,
- sudden outbursts of anger, hostility and aggression,
- explosive screaming and shouting,
- self-harming behaviour,
- rejection of one's body,

- rejection of one's gender role as a man or woman,
- fear of orgasm,
- inability to form partner relationships,
- lack of respect for personal boundaries and shamelessness,
- promiscuity,
- prostitution,
- lying, cheating, keeping secrets,
- delinquency and criminality,
- states of confusion with delusions,
- feeling like you're about to go crazy.

These symptoms make sense, if you know, for instance:

- that the perpetrator always came to the child's bed at night,
- that oral, anal or genital penetration has occurred,
- that the body was forcibly crushed and contorted,
- that the victim's sexual arousal was brought about by force,
- that the victim has been convinced by the perpetrator that nothing bad had happened to her,
- that she was threatened with death if she resists or tells others anything.

The physical symptoms can be the direct result of injuries of the body during sexual violence. They can also be caused by the chronic stress reactions that accompany sexual trauma victims throughout their lives (Banzhaf, 2018; Biedermann, 2018).

Self-harming behaviour

This is a particularly obvious symptom of sexual trauma, when victims engage in self-injury; when they cut themselves with razor blades, knives or scissors or put out burning cigarettes on their hands, or even swallow pieces of glass or razor blades. There can be different underlying motivations for this:

- to overcome their own numbed feelings,
- to relieve the internal pressure,

- to make themselves unattractive to the perpetrator,
- to act out their identification with the perpetrator ('You're just a piece of shit!'),
- to live out anger, hatred and contempt against themselves.

Self-injury is also a non-verbal cry for help from victims of sexual violence. They express their victimhood before the eyes of others, but usually have the experience that no one really understands their message. They are patched-up, their bleeding hands and arms are bandaged, their stomach is pumped out repeatedly. They are admonished and told to pull themselves together and not to do it again. But they will have to do it again and again as long as the sexual trauma is not recognised and addressed and if the perpetrator is not prevented from continuing the sexual trauma. Self-harming behaviour will not end until the full extent and the reason of the suffering of the person comes to light in trauma therapy.

Eating disorders

The same applies to so-called 'eating disorders', which in my experience are very often a result of sexual psychotrauma. Sexually traumatised girls and boys refuse to eat because they suffer from permanent nausea because of the rape and assault. They lose body weight, getting thinner and thinner until they are just skin and bone and are in danger of dehydration and starving to death. They are completely split off from their bodies and live only in their fantasy world. They want to get rid of their body because it feels bad and disgusting to them. Having a body means that they can still be sexually stimulated by perpetrators. They would prefer to lead a completely disembodied existence.

Some do eat but throw up afterwards (Bulimia). Others gorge themselves with vast quantities of different foods all in a very short space of time, then stick their finger in their throat and vomit it up again. Based on my therapeutic experiences they are re-enacting oral rape.

Other victims of sexual violence eat a lot to develop a body armour, which they hope will make them unattractive to the perpetrator and keep him at bay. The layer of fat around them is supposed to help them to feel the attacks less.

A woman who was doing therapy with me showed me photos of herself as a child, in which she had an age-appropriate weight. When the sexual traumatisation by her father began, she became fat and clumsy within a short time.

As the following example shows, food can also serve to ground yourself when the survival parts want to disappear and leave the body forever.

Heavy weight

"The more I wanted to disappear, the more eating took over my wanting to exist. My whole day was focused on food. Hunger was hunger for staying alive. I kept putting on more weight, I became fatter and heavier, until I weighed almost 120 kilos. I was 37 years old and could hardly move." (Kersten, 2018 p. 313)

When such children, adolescents and young women and men are diagnosed with 'anorexia nervosa', 'bulimia' or 'obesity', these pseudoscientific terms conceal the true causes of their symptoms of suffering. Since underneath they have no problem with eating, it is completely absurd to torment them in psychosomatic clinics with cooking courses, diet advice or weight gain measures. What they really need is expert staff to help them unravel the meaning behind their symptoms and survival strategies, to bring their sexual traumatisation, and their entire trauma biography that goes with it, to light. Unfortunately, doctors, psychologists or social pedagogues often side with the traumatising parents; they see 'the anorexic' or 'the overweight child' as the apparent problem of the family. In this way the splits in the psyche of those affected are deepened even further.

Mental 'illnesses'?

At this point I would like to make an urgent appeal to my colleagues in psychiatry: in my experience psychotrauma, and especially the whole field that includes sexual trauma, is the primary underlying cause of those symptoms that psychiatry diagnoses as 'severe mental illnesses'. This is also the reason why trauma victims, and trauma perpetrators, sometimes end up locked up in psychiatric wards and treated against their will. By giving diagnoses such as 'anxiety disorder', 'obsessive-compulsive disorder', 'borderline personality disorder', 'narcissistic personality disorder', 'schizophrenia', 'psychosis', 'dissociative identity disorder', 'sociopathy' or 'psychopathy' and so on, the system of biologically-oriented psychiatry ignores the trauma-background that lies behind such groups of symptoms. The tendency in psychiatry is to pretend that the traumatic event is merely a secondary factor, and that the supposed 'mental illness' is actually caused by 'genes' or an apparent 'impaired cerebral metabolism'. As a result, the human psyche is not taken seriously! Patients are not seen as trauma victims with desperate victim survival strategies. Consequently, no adequate help is given to them (Duncker and Hirschelmann, 2018). In my opinion, the use of psycho-pharmaceutical drugs as a treatment of so-called mental illnesses is in itself a psychotrauma survival strategy imposed by the supposed experts.

At the same time, this system protects the perpetrators of trauma. Because of its approach to 'mental illnesses', psychiatry maintains the inner psychological splits of those affected, and may even reinforce them, and causes the 'patients' further physical damage through the side effects of the medication administered. This then systematically conceals a society-wide scandal, because it hides the full extent of sexual trauma in societies (Ruppert, 2019).

In Germany it is estimated that one in every four, or even as much as one in three, women have experienced sexual violence at some point in their life. 5 to 15 % of all men are also victims of sexual trauma. Since I have ended up travelling worldwide with my seminars, I see that the topic of sexual psychotrauma occurs in every society. It is a daily occurrence in many families, as a side-effect of wars and civil strife, and has been a common practice for many generations. The topic is concealed, denied and swept under the carpet everywhere in the world. The victims of sexual trauma are forced to remain silent, and they themselves very often are seen to be the guilty ones. They experience no loyalty from their families, no protection from the police and only rarely get satisfaction from judiciary systems. Meanwhile, the perpetrators are systematically protected from prosecution. An example: "The lives of two thirds of Mexican women over the age of 15 are saturated with violence. In many cases, abuse begins in childhood." (Süddeutsche Zeitung, 2018, p. 14)

Violence or seduction?

A trauma of sexuality can occur when our own sexuality is used to avoid feeling alone, and to nourish the illusion of being physically touched and loved, and thus feel a right to exist. When sexual psychotrauma takes place during childhood, the initiative for sexual contact comes from the perpetrator. It may begin with caressing, kissing and cuddling, but even when the child is the one doing these things, the initiative and responsibility not to go further always rests with the perpetrator. Such a perpetrator, like his victim, has normally also suffered a trauma of identity and a trauma of love.

Because the victim of sexual violence has to struggle with these two prior forms of trauma herself, she has to go along with the perpetrator's illusion of confusing sexual assault and violence with affection and love. The perpetrator presents himself to his victim as her saviour, who protects her from the violence of others (e.g. her mother or father if they are not the actual perpetrators). He tries to make enforced sexual acts palatable to his victim, depicting them as love and desire. In reality, of course, he draws the victim into his own trauma survival strategies and demands his sexual satisfaction as the price for the 'loving' contact. This is painful for the victim, and deeply shameful, even if she does feel some warmth from the skin contact, sexual excitement and pleasant feelings. That a genital, oral or anal rape is 'nice' or 'fun' is pure imagination on the part of the trauma perpetrator, who would like his victim to see it the same way.

This seduction scenario, which is probably associated with the majority of all sexual psychotraumas, must be distinguished from the brutal violence scenario. Here the perpetrator lives out his delusion of physically and psychologically destroying the victim through the sexual act. In these cases there will be no illusions in the victim of being loved by the perpetrator.

Sex as a Psychotrauma Survival Strategy

Sometimes it seems to me the exception when someone who asks me for therapeutic support has *not* suffered sexual trauma in their childhood. This applies to both women and men. The epidemic and global scale of sexual traumatisation raises the question of how normal our experiences of sexuality really are:

- How extensively is our sexuality fed by illusions and misconceptions of love?
- How far is sexuality just an attempt to cover up our loneliness?
- To what extent is sexuality supposed to compensate for a lack of self-esteem?
- How often is sexuality just an attempt to gain short-term relief from the permanent stress of an individual's lifestyle?
- How often is sex practised with no regard for physical injury or infection?
- How carelessly is sexual intercourse practised without considering the risk of unwanted pregnancies?
- How often is 'true masculinity' or 'true femininity' used as a template for a pseudo-identity in order to avoid feeling one's own childhood traumas?
- How healthy are sexual practices in the respective hetero-, homo-, bi- and transsexual milieux?

Sexuality, when it is practiced as a psychotrauma survival strategy, does not connect us with another human being, it only leads us further into personal isolation. Having sex is sometimes even used on purpose to escape into dissociative states.

Sex for dissociation

A participant in one of my seminars said: "I enjoy sex because it puts me in a dissociative state. I then separate from my body and go into a completely white space where I feel good".

Given the enormous extent of traumatisation in many societies, it is not surprising that sexuality is a form of addiction, used like a drug on a massive scale. It is also often practised in combination with alcohol and drugs.

Based on the example below of a sexually traumatised woman, the following became clear to me:

Legalise surviving!

The legalisation of cannabis is a social attempt to normalise another much used psychotrauma survival strategy. This woman had moved from her country of origin, Romania, to the Netherlands specifically because she could use cannabis there with impunity to numb her trauma feelings.

Drug use can serve both perpetrators and victims – both can apologise afterwards, saying that they had a mental blackout, cannot remember anything and are not responsible for what happened. Even if there may be no conscious memories, and the person's survival strategies do everything to ensure there are no memories, these trauma memories are always seared into the bodies of perpetrators and victims. In their healthy psychological structures, perpetrators too are disgusted by their actions, and so they have to split off from themselves. In extreme cases, a body disconnected from the head has sex with a head without a body. Often it is men who have long since lost and given up all contact with their bodies who practise thoughtless and irresponsible sex with women.

Most people are looking for love and good physical contact. But sexuality on its own can only produce lust. Love can only develop in a relationship, and so sex without relationship is just a flash in the pan. Lust, then, must be repeatedly ignited in order to generate some warmth, but that warmth can only last for a short moment. After a climax without love and real contact many people feel even more empty than before, because now they really feel their loneliness. However, emotional closeness actually frightens them because of their early traumatisation, and so they cannot simply switch themselves on to real relationship, and they must remain lonely, constantly numbing their pain and seeking salvation in increasing forms of self-pleasure. Instead of lust, they actually end up experiencing pain, shame and disgust. In this way they have returned to the starting point that they actually do not want to admit: their deeply painful primary experience of not being wanted, loved and protected by their mother and father.

Partnerships based on Sexual Trauma

If two traumatised people find each other as partners, it is quite possible that in the initial phase of their relationship they experience sexual highlights and have all sorts of variations of intensive sexual intercourse with each other. However, it is often the case that sexually traumatised women activate the survival strategies they developed during their childhood, in order to satisfy their partners and make them dependent on them. These women then appear to their partners as women they have always dreamed about, who are ready for sex at any time and fulfil all their sexual wishes. However, these women have sex in a dissociated state, in which their healthy 'I' and 'want' are somewhere far away. If they orgasm, they psychologically leave their body. Even if there are regular outbreaks of violence within such a partnership, sex enables those concerned to continue with the relationship and maintain the illusion of connection.

In such relationships many men are not with themselves during sex either. They want to impress with their penis and their physical strength. They want to prove that they can bring a woman to orgasm, so that this woman can't help but be like a sexual slave to them. They are all the more frustrated when, after a while, their partner no longer succeeds in mobilising her survival parts for sexual intercourse and instead other parts that find sex disgusting push into the foreground and she cannot bear the physical closeness of a man any longer. These men then no longer understand the world and become angry and aggressive. Some then start to beat their wives and rape them.

Re-staging

Due to the psychological splitting processes, all forms of psychotrauma run a high risk of repeated re-enaction. Since the psychotraumas themselves are repressed, and the survival strategies lose contact with reality, real dangers are not recognised, risks are over- or underestimated, all precautionary measures are neglected and warnings are thrown to the wind. Obvious perpetrators are not seen, and perpetrators are seen where there are none.

As if nothing had happened

Recently I read in a newspaper report that an older woman who was collecting bottles at night to earn some money was raped by four young men. She went to the police and the four men were arrested. A few days later she went out again to collect bottles at night. Because she does not allow the reality of the trauma she has suffered to reach her, she cannot perceive the reality of the risk and continues as if nothing had happened.

Some women lack the intuition when on dating sites that could tell them at first glance if a man is an impostor and liar, only interested in exploiting them financially, emotionally and physically. As in their childhood, such women could not see who is the good 'daddy' and who is the one who emotionally drained them and even physically raped them.

Prostitution, too, is a sphere of society in которых sexual trauma is systematically and daily staged anew. Amongst women who work as prostitutes there is hardly anyone

- who did not have sexual trauma in their childhood;
- who had not already learned, as a small girl, to go into submission, and hope that the perpetrator would rescue her from her loneliness and lack of loving contact from their mother.

In this respect, being at the mercy of a man's sexual desires as a prostitute is a repetition of the survival strategies already known to her from her childhood. Both male and female prostitutes are likely to have been made victims of sexual trauma since childhood. The fact that they get money for their 'work' can be a pattern already learned in childhood.

For 50 pennies

A woman regularly received 50 pennies from her grandpa whenever she sexually satisfied him. As a young woman she then earned money in a massage studio and also satisfied men if they asked for masturbation. She could only admit that her grandfather had actually penetrated her vaginally after many years of therapy.

Some prostitutes may see themselves no longer as helpless and at the mercy of others. In contrast to their childhood situation, it is as if they can now decide for themselves how far a man can go with them and how much money they can demand for it. This is why some prostitutes self-confidently claim that they want to do what they do and that they enjoy it. Meanwhile, there are prostitution lobby groups in Germany who have managed to create a prostitution law that states that prostitution is an occupation (sex work) like any other. As a result, Germany has become a magnet for international sex tourism and the criminal shadow world of prostitution.

The fatal consequences of this law were shown in a television documentary called 'Bordell Deutschland' (ZDF, 2017). What impressed me about this film was an interview with a young woman who managed to get out of prostitution after she had read on the leaflet of an aid organisation that prostitution is a traumatisation. She then was able to establish a relationship with herself on the basis of the symptoms described in the text and afterwards she sought appropriate trauma-therapeutic help.

As a rule, a visit to a brothel is a re-staging of trauma for the clients too. Anyone who goes to a dominatrix – someone who physically torments and verbally humiliates them – has already experienced the same thing as a child. The dominatrix represents the rejecting and unreachable mother who, due to her own sexual traumatisation, cannot physically let the child get close to her, and despises male sexuality.

I experienced this with a man who worked as a medical doctor. He was married and father of a child, but he still compulsively went to a dominatrix. He risked everything: his professional career and his marriage. The same applies to the man in the following example.

In the toilet

Recently I read a newspaper report about a sports trainer who had installed cameras in the ceiling of the toilets of a sports club. He had filmed naked girls and boys over many years. For me this sparked the question: what forms of traumatisation does this man carry within him in order to have to pursue this compulsive voyeurism, which now, when everything has come to light, will ruin his entire life?

When people act from their trauma survival strategies, everything they do is pointless. They blindly re-stage their own victim experiences, and by doing so they switch from the role of victim to perpetrator. They are trying to erase their experiences of powerlessness and pain by victimising others. For a short period of time they have the illusion of power, control over others, intimate closeness or even love. But this only further damages their own psyche, increasing the feelings of guilt, shame and disgust in themselves to an intolerable extent. It is simply disgusting when men manage their sexual arousal by having sexual intercourse with children, and these men, in their healthy parts, know this. Otherwise, prisoners known as 'child fuckers' would not be at the bottom of the prison hierarchy.

Stalking

Women are sometimes 'stalked' by men who will not let them go, even if the woman has ended the relationship, or never even had a relationship with the man. Perpetrators instinctively sense the powerless child parts in their victims and do not let them go as long as the victims still feel their fear. For the perpetrators, pursuing a victim is a trauma survival strategy: the excitement and thrill of the chase stops them having to feel their own split-off trauma anxieties. If these women then turn to the police or aid organisations after a long period of suffering, these organisations may impose contact bans on the stalkers, or the persecuted woman may be given practical tips and advice on how to behave, or she may be supported in court. Such victims of persecution may not find peace even if they change their place of residence and move far away from the stalker: in these times of the internet and social media, stalkers can easily make themselves reappear in their victim's consciousness and continue to scare and terrify them. The following case study shows how important it is for victims of stalking to be able to protect themselves from their persecutors by looking at their trauma biography.

Self-protection

In my experience, stalking for the victim is a repetition of their childhood situation. As a child they experienced powerlessness and were unable to protect themselves from a perpetrator. This happened to Anna, whose father sexually traumatised her as a child. When she told her mother about it, her mother did not want to know anything about it and called her a liar. When Anna was able to figure this out for herself in a therapy session, she suddenly recognised the connection and understood why her countless requests for help from those around her to protect her from a stalker, just as in her childhood, were not heard and not successful. At the end of this hour of therapy, she was determined to defend herself. This time she was successful. The stalking stopped.

Trauma perpetrators

Perpetrators who sexually traumatise other people are mostly male. They are partners, husbands, internet acquaintances, fathers, stepfathers, grandfathers, uncles, educators, priests, teachers, doctors, psychotherapists, superiors, colleagues, etc. They can also be male children or adolescents who re-stage their own trauma of sexuality with their playmates, sisters, nieces, housemates etc.

It can be assumed that people who sexually traumatise other people have experienced something similar, although this is not always the case. In their identity however they are always traumatised and trapped in a trauma of love.

Perpetrators may also be female, if they are mothers, aunts, educators, teachers or superiors. Two cases of maternal perpetration, one against a daughter and one against a son, were impressively described in a German television documentary (ARD, 2012). The programme showed how the mothers gradually eroticised their relationship with their son or daughter, and increasingly seduced their children into sexual acts, coercing them by force. Each child was so strongly emotionally bound to their mother by the fear she made them feel and the aggression she showed to them, that it was impossible for them to break free from entanglement with her. Unfortunately the trauma background of the mothers was not explored in the programme. However, I am sure that both women carry within them the entire spectrum of a psychotrauma biography.

Because mothers are directly involved with their children's genital area when changing nappies and during personal hygiene, their sexual assaults are not so easily noticed. These mothers may be sexually aroused, and get flashbacks that have to do with their own sexual trauma. They then may commit acts with their own child that they themselves suffered as children.

The fact that some women are perpetrators of sexual violence is a highly taboo subject. One seldom believes their victims when they speak of their experiences (Homes, 2004). For this reason the number of cases of female perpetrators is probably massively underestimated; it could well be that as much as 20% of sexual perpetrators are women. In addition, male victims are faced with the dilemma of defining themselves as a victim, since it is part of general male self-image to always see sex as something good, something of which a man cannot get enough (Bange, 2007).

Something that cannot have happened

I recently learnt how an expert had rejected a man's application for payment after an extensive and costly psychological report under the Victim Compensation Act. This man, with whom I had worked therapeutically for a while, showed all the signs of a psychotrauma biography. According to his account, he had been blackmailed by his mother into regular sexual intercourse since the onset of puberty. On the assumption that if something should not have happened, and is beyond our comprehension, then it cannot have happened, the expert concluded that it could not be ruled out that this was all the man's imagining. According to the 'expert', he suffered from fictitious memories, and these 'memories' had been confirmed by his therapists in the mistaken belief that the 'abuse' by his mother had actually taken place.

> *Even detailed descriptions by the man as to the time and place of sexual contact with his mother were ignored, with reference made to the alleged scientific research into 'false memories'. In my view, it would be a minimum of scientific honesty to say that, as an outside person, you cannot know what actually happened to someone else. Only the person who actually experienced it can remember that. To claim with the stamp of scientific authority that the whole thing did not take place, and only occurred in the imagination of the person concerned, is in my opinion, a (co-) perpetration in the guise of science.*

Not to believe a victim of sexual trauma forms, in addition to the act itself, a fundamental basis for his psychotrauma, from which he may suffer for the rest of his life.

Even if a mother does not become an actual sexual perpetrator herself, she may be close by when her child is sexually traumatised by another person. If she leaves her child alone, looks away and does not protect him or her, she allows the perpetration to take place. For example, perhaps she does not want to see what is really happening when her older son harasses and sexually uses a younger sister. She may even call her daughter a 'whore' if she does dare to talk about the sexual assaults. This betrayal by one's own mother is often experienced as even more painful than the physical assaults themselves by those affected.

A good example of this is the documentary film 'No Lullaby' (German Title: 'Nirgendland' 2014).

Abuse over several generations

> *The film 'No Lullaby' is an impressive document of how a mother who was sexually traumatised by her father did not realise what her father then also did to her own daughter for almost ten years. Her own mother, who was raped by Russian soldiers after the Second World War, had given her the advice: "If you scream, you will be killed. When you grow up and get married, all this will be forgotten". This film is also the chronicle of a judicial scandal in*

which the perpetrator was not sentenced, when accused by his granddaughter, in spite of overwhelming evidence. The granddaughter then committed suicide shortly after the trial.

Mother Terror

Mothers who were sexually traumatised as children, and who suppress and deny this, exert a tremendous psychological terror on their families through their victim attitudes. They often despise their husbands, get angry and flip out, are depressed for days or lie in bed plagued by nameless illnesses. They often threaten to commit suicide. They are not predictable for their children, who have to be on their guard all the time. What will my mother do next? When will she suddenly switch again and overwhelm me with protestations of love, portraying herself as a caring mother, dragging me to doctors, having concerned conversations with my teachers about me, etc.? Neither children nor husbands have a chance against her trauma survival strategies.

Trauma perpetrator attitudes

The forms of sexual traumatisation against children allow conclusions about the survival strategies of the perpetrators (both male and female). Some perpetrators behave in a passive dependent manner, stressing to the child victim how bad they feel, how much they need the child's attention and love, and how sexual stimulation and satisfaction can help them get better again. Perpetrators of this kind regress into a childlike state, putting the child above themselves as an authority figure. They thereby evoke the child's care and compassion. Probably this is the more frequent variant, especially in the case of sexual traumatisation within families. The perpetrators move from their trauma-victim attitudes into the position of the perpetrator through phrases like:

- "Please be kind to me!"
- "Look how poorly I am."

- "You can make me feel better again!"
- "I love you and you love me!"
- "Nothing bad has happened."
- "What we're doing here is our secret!"
- "You don't want your father to go to prison, do you?"

To describe this group of perpetrators as 'paedophiles' is confusing, because this Greek word means 'lover of children', but there is no healthy love here. There are only illusions of love born out of the perpetrator's own trauma of love as a child, which make the perpetrators themselves believe that they love the children whom, in truth, they hurt and cause severe emotional damage for the rest of their lives. Children are easy prey for them. They do not fight back, are easily intimidated and can be satisfied with small rewards. This would be much more difficult with adults.

Just cuddling?

A sexual trauma perpetrator explained his assaults on his daughter in the following way: "I had my first sexual encounter with my youngest daughter (now ten) when she was three. She came to me and snuggled up, cuddled and stroked me. That was very pleasant for me. At that time she was the active one, and I did not say no because it was beautiful. That went on for several years, then she suddenly did not want it anymore. When she fended it off, although she continued to cuddle up to me in bed, on the sofa, watching TV, it was not easy for me to accept. I think I did nothing explicitly against her will. I may have harassed her with my attempted advances towards the end.

"She is still nice and sociable. If she is with me now after my divorce from her mother, she sometimes lies down in my bed to sleep. My feeling is that no trauma has arisen in her because of this."

The term 'sexual encounter' in the above example just shows how many miles away from the reality of their victims, sexual trauma perpetrators can be. The following report, for example, shows how it really is for their victims:

Muscle cramps

"I am in my early 60s, and over the course of my life with the help of two forms of therapy, I have reclaimed some of the parts of me that I had split-off. Above all, accessing my anger again was of enormous importance to me. As the daughter of a mother incapable of love, who openly rejected me emotionally, I had shouldered the guilt of the whole world and had not been able to build up a particularly high self-esteem. My father, on whom I was emotionally dependent, got into bed with me from the age of five to twelve.

"Apart from vague body memories and nocturnal muscle cramps, I have no memory of this. Besides, I had no idea of it until my mid-forties and would always have said that while my brother fled to our mother's bed, I did not want my father in bed with me.

"It was in a conversation with my parents that I learned that this had actually taken place. I had attacked my mother and she wanted to distract from herself and put the focus onto my father by telling me this. With this discovery, which was totally new to me, I reacted as an uninvolved person and only realised much later what had come to light."

The tactic of being a needy victim who is constantly looking for sympathy is also used by adult perpetrators against adult women.

Perpetrators can also appear in the aggressive-dominant form. Because of their own trauma biography, their own unwanted, unloved and unprotected existence, they carry anger, hatred and self-denial within them, and transfer these feelings of trauma onto the outside world. They see in their victims those parts of them that they themselves have split off and would like to erase. They fight their own traumatised parts vicariously through another person, insulting them, punishing them and inflicting on them what was done to them by a perpetrator. They hate this completely innocent person, will hurt them and may actually destroy them. They imitate the perpetrator attitudes that they themselves had to experience when they were in the position of victim:

- "It's my right and your duty to have sex with me!"
- "I was the one who paid for it!"
- "I am your father/I'm the breadwinner!"
- "You seduced me!"
- "Don't be like that: It is beautiful and not bad for you!"
- "Even if you say no and defend yourself, in reality you mean yes!"
- "Nobody will believe you because you are a liar!"

This group of perpetrators also does not shy away from drugging their victims, plying them with alcohol, beating them first or making death threats against them before raping them. Their language is brutal and crude. They talk about 'fresh meat', for example, which they are 'horny for'.

Rehder and Meilinger (1997) have tried to classify male offenders convicted of 'sexual abuse' into different types. They came to the following conclusion, which supports my differentiation of trauma survival strategies that fall into predominantly victim or perpetrator attitudes. Accordingly, trauma perpetrators are either

- depressive, with a readiness to adapt;
- socially adjusted and obsessively structured;
- adjusted, then periodically uninhibited by alcohol;
- socially competent, cast aside from normal life, in denial of actions, or ...
- criminally entrenched and recklessly egocentric.

The Trauma of Sexuality

It is particularly easy for perpetrators to commit crimes against children that are not wanted, not loved and so not protected by their parents. These children are hungry for attention and physical contact, and so are easily seduced. They sometimes may even lead other victims to the perpetrator, as Karl Grünberg illustrates in an article about a sexual trauma perpetrator who perpetrated against at least 11 boys in 379 individual acts of sexual trauma (Grünberg, 2018). One of the many reasons why boys in particular do not speak of what they have suffered is their fear of possibly being considered 'gay'.

The principle of perpetrator attitudes consists in reversing the facts:

- Truths spoken by the victim are called lies.
- One's own lies are asserted as definitive truths.
- One's own dirty actions are attributed to the victim: You are dirty!
- When the victim reveals the truth about the perpetrator's sordid actions in the family, she is named a traitor.
- The perpetrator justifies his own aggression as self-defence against the behaviour of his victim.
- If the victim defends herself, she is called aggressive.
- The victim's traumatisation is reinterpreted as support and help for which the victim should be grateful.
- The perpetrator sees himself as the unfortunate victim of his victim's behaviour.

Trauma Victim Attitudes

Since most victims of sexual traumatisation do not want to admit to their victimhood, and cannot bear it psychologically and emotionally, they develop victim attitudes that function according to the same principle of perpetrator-victim reversal:

- I am fine, it was nothing.
- My father, grandpa ... would never do something like this, I am just imagining it.

- My grandpa, daddy, teacher ... loves me.
- I have to make even more of an effort to be a good child.
- It is my responsibility to make sure my mum does not kill herself.
- I am in charge of ensuring that we are a healthy family.
- It is my fault that this happened to me.
- I should be ashamed.
- I had lustful feelings myself.
- I am bad, sinful, depraved.
- I deserve it.
- My body is there for that purpose.
- I must not tell anyone anything, otherwise my daddy, grandpa ... will go to prison.

In this respect perpetrator and victim attitudes go well together, which is why sexual traumatisation can be undiscovered for many years. Some victims may even regret it when the perpetrator turns away from them and moves on to another victim. Inner parts of them then feel rejected and no longer loved. They are disappointed when they realise that the perpetrator is doing the same thing with other children, since they thought that they were special to him. The trauma survival strategies of victims and perpetrators hold together with a tenacity that is difficult to comprehend in everyday reality, so making it difficult to bring the atrocities to an end.

Perpetrator strategies

Anita Heiliger (2000) has evaluated court documents to understand how convicted 'abusers' operate. She came to the following conclusions:

- The perpetrators initially develop strategies to get closer to and make contact with their child victims. They are friendly and kind, responding to the needs of their victim, become beloved playmates and doing special things with the child, who does not otherwise get to experience such things.

- The next step is to develop strategies that allow access to the victim. The perpetrator tries to make himself indispensable, e.g. he assumes parental responsibilities (homework supervision, looking after the child when the parents are absent), which the parents experience as a relief.
- Then perpetrators try to break up the relationship their victim has to those who would potentially protect them. They draw their victim over to their side, and devalue their proper guardians: "Your mother doesn't understand you!" The worse the victim's relationship to these people becomes – in the case of the child their primary caregivers – the easier it is for the perpetrator. Step by step, the perpetrator puts himself in the position of an emotional attachment figure for his victim. If this trap snaps shut on the child, the perpetrator has an easy time from now on.
- The sexual assaults are increased gradually: the perpetrator photographs the child; he rubs himself up against the child whilst they are both fully clothed; the perpetrator asks the child to undress; bathroom doors are no longer allowed to be locked; the child must watch the perpetrator masturbate; the perpetrator asks the child to satisfy him orally; the perpetrator penetrates the child orally, anally or genitally.

In her study Heiliger found that perpetrators often continued to weave their strategies even after their deeds had been uncovered. They then tried to exonerate themselves and shift the responsibility for their actions away from themselves. In court for example, they say that they can not remember anything, refer to alcohol or drug consumption, trivialise the issue and, if necessary, blame the victim for having seduced them into such actions. Some admit certain incidents in court in order to cover up others that were even worse. They give the impression of cooperation in front of the judge and the public prosecutor, feigning insight and remorse in order to get a milder sentence. If they get this, they usually continue with their perpetration, if possible even seeking out the same victim, or immediately searching for a new one.

Even in prisons or in the correctional system, perpetrators continue their strategies of ensnaring and entangling victims for sexual trauma. This could be a prison officer or a social worker or a psychologist. There are documented cases where female prison wardens have helped such perpetrators escape (SRF Swiss Radio, 2016). There are records of brutal cases where trauma perpetrators take a woman hostage in prison and rape her for hours.

People who have similar trauma backgrounds intuitively attract each other. Networks of perpetrators, needing their perpetrator attitudes to avoid falling into the abyss of their trauma feelings, are created in civil society, in the penal system and in the forensic sector. Such perpetrators can unerringly detect people who are trauma victims and who escape into victim attitudes, and these trauma victims are themselves unconsciously drawn to trauma perpetrators.

Anita Heiliger's findings about the extent and persistence of perpetrator strategies, and the associated perpetrator-victim dynamics in relationships confirm my thesis that perpetrators of 'sexual abuse' are themselves severely traumatised. They can only stop their perpetrator survival strategies if they work through their own psychotrauma biography. The efforts of police investigations, court proceedings, probation officers, social work, conventional psychotherapies, criminal punishment and imprisonment are of little use to a society if this does not happen. None of these can really change anything in a lasting way or prevent sex trauma perpetrators from carrying on with their crimes. The police and judiciary, who know nothing about the dynamics of psychotrauma, cannot effectively protect a society from further acts of violence.

The Staufen im Breisgau case[10]

A case of sexual traumatisation in Germany, which in 2018 caused a great stir in the media (Süddeutche Zeitung 2018; all literal quotations are taken from this article) is a horrendous example of the futility of prosecution, sentencing, social work or psychotherapy,

- when the focus is only on combating symptoms, and
- if the psychotraumas in the perpetrators are not recognised and named as such and nothing is changed in relation to their trauma biography.

A 47-year-old mother gave her nine-year-old son over to a 38-year-old man, who had courted her with his flatteries to get at her child. She eventually let this man offer her son to other men for sexual traumatisation through the Darknet, and they both made a lot of money out of it. She was present when her son was raped (numerous times) in her own apartment. This happened for two years before the criminal investigation department managed to blow the whistle and arrest the perpetrator in a bogus handover of the child to customers.

This case is particularly disturbing because the mother (Mrs T) had been known to the social services and the courts for a considerable time, and the perpetrator (Mr L) had been the subject of police attention for many years because of his possession of child pornography.

Mr L had been given a suspended sentence of one year and later had been imprisoned for many years for repeated offences. He continued to use his freedom to collect child pornographic material on his computer, distributing it, and making pornographic films with a 13-year-old girl. When the authorities found out about him again and confiscated his computer, he got a new one the same day. He was sentenced to four years and four months imprisonment for his continued offending. Because he cooperated in court – made a supposedly credible confession, and allegedly wanted to be treated – the judge waived the preventative detention requested by the public prosecutor's office after serving his prison sentence. The judge wanted to help the offender return to a normal life. She told him in court: "You deserve a second chance."

The perpetrator took full advantage of this renewed opportunity to continue his criminal activities. While in prison, he talked to other prisoners about their sexual preferences and wrote an essay steeped in pornographic and sadistic fantasies.

Since he was classified as 'high risk' of reoffending after his time in prison, he was placed under supervision. He had to maintain regular contact with police officers as part of a programme for sex offenders at high risk of reoffending, in addition to starting therapy in a forensic outpatient clinic and staying away from minors.

Nevertheless, he soon met Mrs T, the mother (Mrs T) of his former victim, moved in with her, played the caring father for the boy, presenting himself as better for the child than his overburdened mother who had little interest in him. He pulled out all the stops of his perpetrator strategies described above towards the mother and the child: "I definitely do care about the child", "The boy likes what happened!" Mr L only attended the prescribed therapy sessions irregularly, just wanting the 40 minutes to go by as quickly as possible so that he could then go back to continue his sexual assaults for the next two or three weeks. The psychotherapist who was supposed to work with him obviously did not have a concrete therapeutic goal, and he was not aware that Mr L was again committing sexual assaults. He even assumed that the perpetrator had formed a positive bond with the boy who was his victim, and that this would help the boy with his healthy development. Therefore the psychotherapist wrote a letter of recommendation on official notepaper at the perpetrator's request, certifying that he did not pose any danger to his girlfriend's child.

The perpetrator carefully maintained contact with the police officers and the probation officer. "He tries to do everything right," his probation officer said. He obviously wanted to make sure that nobody found out and realised what he was actually doing. For a long time, the police and probation officers did not know that Mr L had contact with Mrs T and her son, and was again collecting child pornography on his computer. He even uploaded videos he made with the boy and the daughter of one of Mrs T's friends to the Darknet and sold them there. The sexual assaults on the boy became more and more frequent and violent over time. He was sold to four different men. Fifty cases of abuse against the boy ended up being indicted. Even the

Youth Welfare Office had noticed that the perpetrator was in the mother's apartment, contrary to police regulations, and was therefore in contact with a minor. A team made an unannounced house visit, and made Mrs T & Mr L promise that Mr L would no longer be allowed to stay in the apartment in the presence of the boy. But in reality this had no effect. So a short time later the Youth Welfare Office took the boy into care and placed him with a foster family. When the mother objected in court to the boy being taking into custody, apparently credibly playing the role of the desperate mother in front of the family court and the Youth Welfare Office, the boy returned to her home. The judge at the family court said afterwards: "Because she hadn't dressed up specially, she seemed to me authentic and genuine. 'Look, I don't need to make myself beautiful, I am who I am. I love my son, he loves me'." According to the judge, the mother appeared very convincing and forceful. The judge was surprised at the discrepancy between the person herself and her torrent of words. The boy's ordeal continued.

For me, this is a good example of how inadequate the everyday psychological understanding of judges is to sufficiently comprehend psychotrauma and psychotrauma survival strategies. In my experience, a lot of chatter is, in itself, an unmistakable sign that people are under trauma pressure and are trying to talk away their chronic hyper-agitation. They cannot even listen to and reflect on what others are saying to them. Their manic talking is an attempt to quieten their inner turmoil and to block out the influence of others to what they are doing. Traumatised people, even those with low intelligence, show an enormous will to survive. The more traumatised they are, the more unstoppable are their survival strategies.

Impressively, Michaela Huber (2018) points out in an article in 'Stern' magazine that mothers are people who, because of their own history, are capable of every cruelty, even towards their own children. The 'mother myth' that all mothers love their children should no longer be used to close our eyes to the reality of mothers as perpetrators.

In this Staufen im Breisgau case, due to her easy experiences with the courts, the perpetrator-mother went on and even tried at the relevant higher regional court to get her son to have a more relaxed contact with the perpetrator.

How traumatised both the perpetrator-mother and her perpetrator-boyfriend are is already clear from the few things known about their biographies: Mrs T's mother died of epilepsy when Mrs T was three years old, and she then went to live with her grandmother, who then died when Mrs T was eleven, and she ended up in the care of her older brother. As is common with severe trauma biographies, the perpetrator-mother can only make a few coherent statements to the experts, because she has an extremely incomplete biographical knowledge, and can hardly describe what was significant in her life. She had difficulty obtaining her secondary school leaving diploma and worked in the nursing profession after a year of voluntary service. At the age of 24 she had her first child, a daughter. After two marriages, she and another man conceived the boy who was later so severely sexually traumatised with her help and in her presence. After the boy's father died early, the mother smoked pot, left her household in a state of neglect, lived on social welfare and worked at various part time jobs. When she met Mr L, she did everything she could to please him, including handing over the daughter of an acquaintance and her own son for sexual exploitation. This is a textbook example of someone stuck in the trauma of love so as not to feel their trauma of identity. For her disorders that were a result of her trauma, which were officially declared 'depressions', a youth welfare officer merely advised her to take medication.

So there is every reason to believe that Mrs T acted most of the time from her psychotrauma survival strategies, and that she never got to form a healthy 'I' and 'want' function because of her early traumatisation. Instead, she fought through life with her survival programmes. By making herself impervious to all references to her own responsibility, she impressed, amongst others, the judges (who do not have any understanding of psychotraumas and what a psychotrauma biography is) with these strategies.

The outright refusal to take oneself seriously, to reflect on and deal with one's behaviour is a typical sign that trauma survival strategies are at work. It is a form of self-immunisation to be able to deny one's traumatisations and not feel all the pain that this entails. Instead, others are found to be guilty for what goes wrong and they are perceived as acting unjustly. Alternating victim attitudes – "I'm sick, I'm depressed!" – and perpetrator attitudes – "I won't let you interfere with my life" are used to struggle through somehow. Where necessary, the person then cooperates with the authorities. But as soon as they sense the possibility of getting the authorities out of their life, they start strategically planning for this and skilfully implementing it. Under such circumstances, children have no chance of being seen with their own needs or to be taken seriously by their mother and protected by her. In view of what Mrs T enacted with her son, I think that it is highly likely that she herself was also sexually traumatised as a child although this was not mentioned in the official reports.

Mr L's life story also reveals a clear psychotrauma biography. According to his mother he was conceived as a result of rape. He does not know his biological father. According to his own statements, he was sexually abused by an uncle at the age of six or seven. When he was nine years old his mother married a violent, alcoholic man. Because of his mother's psychological problems, he was repeatedly put into care. He completed secondary school through the detour of a special needs school. He broke off an apprenticeship as a cook and completed basic military service as a medical orderly. He then became a petty criminal. He lied and cheated, and understood how to skilfully trick other people.

He built up his illusory world, adapted externally and re-staged his trauma biography of being an unwanted, unloved and unprotected child. He has no healthy 'I' at his disposal to tell him what is right and what is wrong. He is constantly under pressure from his traumatised parts, constantly running away from them and his unbearable pain. With his survival strategies he draws new people into his inner chaos: the more traumatised a person is, the more relentlessly and compulsively he functions from his survival strategies.

On 7th August 2018, Mrs T was sentenced to twelve and a half years in prison. Mr L received twelve years in prison with subsequent preventive detention. Yet again, Mr L had managed to get around the judge with his well-practised strategy of cooperation, and so escaped a higher prison sentence. He presented himself in court as the real advocate of law and justice, as if he was the judge, not the perpetrator. Again, the court did not see through his trauma survival strategies and perpetrator attitudes. As the initiator and principal offender, he received a less severe prison sentence than the woman he had dragged into his rapacious madness.

Staufen im Breisgau is by no means an isolated case. There are many others, one of which is the case of a man from Lügde in Westphalia, Germany, which became known in the spring of 2019, where there were multiple grounds for suspicion of sexual traumatisation. This man had lured at least 29 children into his shabby caravan on a campsite and sexually traumatised them. In this case, too, the Youth Welfare Office had known about this for a long time and, as the height of absurdity, even appointed the perpetrator as foster father for a girl who then served as a decoy for other children (Süddeutsche Zeitung, 2019c). He even flagrantly hung up advertising leaflets in a nearby supermarket to lure children into his trap. The ongoing criminal investigation proceedings will be hopefully able to clarify to what extent those within the police department involved in the case were themselves responsible.

These cases alone would be enough to warrant compulsory further training of lawyers (judges, public prosecutors, defence lawyers) in psychotraumatology as a matter of urgency. In addition, the employees of the youth welfare departments, the probation services and associated psychotherapists urgently need basic knowledge about the psychotrauma biography in which most of their clients and patients are trapped. Instead of investing their energy and working time in such absurd undertakings as diagnosing the traumatised child, who has become conspicuous at school, for 'suspected autism', they would then be better able to recognise the victim and perpetrator attitudes of his tormentors earlier. They would then also not let themselves be deceived, lied to and appeased by the perpetrators so easily and with such great naivety. Instead of using blurred terms such as 'difficult childhood' or 'terrible destiny', they would then have unambiguous concepts and a clear standpoint at their disposal in order not to let themselves be entangled in the perpetrator-victim dynamics of such traumatising partnership and family relationship systems.

In conclusion: if you are dealing with traumatised people, you cannot achieve anything substantial if you do not understand psychotrauma. Therefore, the police, the judiciary and assisting professional groups such as doctors, psychologists or social workers cannot adequately protect a society from sexual perpetrators. On the contrary, they actually protect more the perpetrators when they argue in favour of 'victim protection': if the perpetrator confesses, he will receive a mild sentence, because then the victim would be spared the confrontation with the perpetrator. This happened in the case of a 66-year-old deacon who raped a 15-year-old girl who trusted him. He was able to leave the courtroom smiling contentedly with a suspended sentence, while the girl ended up highly traumatised in a psychiatric ward. (Süddeutsche Zeitung, 2019b).

Traumatised society

When two people, as in the cases I've just described, are monitored, cared for, convicted, and given therapy by the state, no one really understands them or offers them an effective way to understand themselves so that they can stop spreading trauma around them in all directions. In an altogether traumatised society, the existence of psychotrauma is the most repressed phenomenon. Psychotraumas are simply ignored or portrayed as extremely rare events, and in this way psychotraumas and their physical, psychological and social consequences are kept alive and constantly recreated with the help of social institutions. In a false 'we', victims and perpetrators fake the illusion of togetherness in order not to have to feel the frightening feelings of guilt and shame within themselves.

Sexual traumatisation can be observed long before any action is taken. However if it is, something is often done that avoids clearly naming the phenomenon of traumatisation in both victims and perpetrators. Instead in traumatised societies we pay more attention to those who speak of the concept of trauma as an exaggeration, an inflationary use of the term, or of false memory and the inadequacies of our memory, urgently warning against believing the memories of trauma victims.

We psychotherapists are often suspected of talking those with whom we work into believing that sexual violence happened to them, and that actually nothing happened and the poor families the patients come from now have to suffer from these monstrous accusations against them (Loftus and Ketcham, 1994; Shaw, 2016).

Of course it is possible that someone may be wrongly suspected and charged as a sex offender. This is probably more likely to happen when a victim of sexual violence suppresses her own traumatisation, thereby protecting the true perpetrator. When this happens, the split-off sexual trauma experiences are then likely to be projected onto her own children. People who only know sexual traumatisation from stories they hear or who only inform themselves about it through literature and without sufficient self-exploration, are at risk of overreaction on the one hand, and of a complete blindness to the trauma on the other. Sometimes they see sexual trauma everywhere and sometimes they see nothing at all.

All men are ...

I experienced this with a man whose wife suspected him of sexual 'abuse' of their daughter. This happened when the daughter reached the age at which the mother had become a victim of sexual assault herself. In this case, the staff of the Youth Welfare Office believed the wife and put the husband under considerable pressure, making custody decisions to his disadvantage. He was condemned as a perpetrator and had to fight hard for his reputation.

It is clearly recommended for employees of the police, the court system and social services to assume that the people they are dealing with are stuck in a psychotrauma biography and cannot free themselves from it on their own. Their 'clients' will continue with their trauma survival strategies in one way or another for as long as they can, even intensifying them, even if they are punished for it.

It does not feel good to have the wool pulled over your eyes by other people's trauma survival strategies. From my perspective it is helpful to notice when another person creates in us a feeling of helplessness and powerlessness, or our contact with them leaves us in a state of considerable confusion. Such resonances are a good indicator for me that this person has split off psychotraumas.

Blind spot

> I can only correctly recognise psychotraumas in other people if I deal with my own psychotraumas. I can certainly say that is true for me. For a long time I did not have the slightest idea of psychotrauma. I could not recognize traumatisations in others even when they happened right in front of me. I could not see beyond my own trauma survival strategies. That is why I thought what others were doing was normal even when their actions were quite extreme survival strategies.

Anyone who does not yet have access to their own sexual trauma will not be able to see it in others either. That person will be blind to the reality of sexual traumatisation around them even if she works in a profession intended to give people clarity about themselves. If she is a psychotherapist, she herself will try to play down the issue and calm her client down: "With the best will in the world, I really can't imagine that what you tell me about your parents is true!" She is inevitably drawn into the whirlpool of confusion of victims and perpetrators, because confusion, in other words not wanting to see reality, is the number one survival strategy for both perpetrators and victims. As long as it remains unclear what happened and is possibly still happening, who does what, who is damaged and who has to endure the damage, it is psychologically not true and it can always be the other way round. The victim and perpetrator attitudes deliberately create such confusion.

It becomes completely crazy in a society when even the institutions whose task it is to prevent sexual traumas are riddled with perpetrators. This happened in Sweden, for example, where an inspector in charge of monitoring lawful behaviour was caught by police officers when he visited a prostitute, which is a punishable offence under Swedish law (Häggström 2016, p. 245 ff.). It can be assumed that this is not an isolated case.

The case of Michael Jackson

What has now come to light concerning the American superstar Michael Jackson is almost inconceivable. In the documentary 'Leaving Neverland' (by Dan Reed), two men talk openly about how their revered idol used all the classic perpetrator strategies that I have described above to draw them gradually into his sex games. It can be assumed that these two men were not isolated cases, but that the superstar, whose own childhood was also traumatising, could always easily get new 'lovers'. What does this say about a society that, blinded by the glamour, fame and wealth of its stars, does not dare to speak the truth, because lawyers are immediately on the scene to gag anyone who threatens such a million-dollar business? What does it say that other celebrities vouch for Michael Jackson, even though they cannot possibly know what really happened? The show must go on – even if it forces countless children and families into misery.

Sexual trauma in art

In poems, novels, songs, pictures and so forth, people express their unconscious inner world, often without being aware of it themselves. Readers, listeners, and viewers likewise receive the artist's works through their own traumatised and survival parts. The traumatised parts will get a sense of what the work is really about, but the survival parts will ignore that reality and distract from it, and elevating it, for example, to an expression of 'art'.

The poem 'The Erlkönig / The Erl-King', for example, is, in my view, the description of the sexual traumatisation of a child by his own father. Here is the poem:[11]

> Who is riding so late through the night and the gale?
> A father clutching his boy so pale;
> He has the lad wrapped in his arm,
> To keep him warm and safe from harm.
>
> 'Son, why do you hide your face in fear?'
> 'Don't you see him, father, the Erl-King's here?
> The Erl-King in his robe and crown.'
> 'It's shapes in the fog, my boy, calm down.'
>
> *'You lovely child, why don't you come with me?*
> *We'll play together and what games they'll be.*
> *On my shores, flowers of such colours grow,*
> *And the dresses my mother has, with gold they glow.'*
>
> 'O father, my father, can't you hear
> These promises he whispers in my ear?'
> 'There, my child, be quiet, be still.
> It's the wind through the dry leaves blowing its chill.'
>
> *'Do you want, my fine boy, to come with me?*
> *My daughters will care for you tenderly.*
> *By night they'll lead you in the dances they leap,*
> *They'll sway and they'll swing and they'll sing you to sleep.'*

> 'O father, my father can't you see them there?
> The Erl-King's daughters in the gloomy air.'
> 'My son, my son all I can see clear
> Is the old trees of willow grey and drear.'
>
> *'I love you, your beautiful body draws me off course.*
> *And if you're not willing, I'll have to use force.'*
> 'O father, my father, he's touching me now
> The Erl-King hurts me, I can't say how.'
>
> The father trembles, he rides without rest,
> He holds the child, who moans at his breast.
> By tooth and by claw, to the farm he sped,
> But clasped tight in his arms, the child was dead.

The child is split in his relationship to the father. The child sees a part of his father as someone who offers him security and shelter. The other part is the seducer, whom the child does not identify as a father, but as a threatening monster. I have experienced this dynamic of splitting in numerous therapy sessions. When the child turns to the protector-father, the father placates and distracts the child. In the end, the child is completely confused and psychologically destroyed.

This makes me ask myself: What happens to schoolchildren who (have to) memorise this poem without being made aware of its traumatic content? What is the effect on them when they see that even obvious descriptions of sexual violence ('And if you're not willing, I'll have to use force') are not named as such by their teachers, and referred to as something in the realm of childish fantasies? Whom can they then turn to when they themselves are in need?

Sexual traumatisation of children in families

Although adults do warn children about the 'bad man' lurking in wait for them around the corner or in the park, the main crime scene for sexual trauma is within the family and the child's immediate surroundings. Sexual traumatisation occurs there in various ways and with different levels of severity:

- There is a sexualised atmosphere in the family; suggestive remarks are made all the time.
- Children are undressed when it is not necessary.
- Children are observed in intimate situations; toilet and bathroom doors are not allowed to be locked.
- The perpetrator fixes his eyes on every area of the child's body and bare skin. (A woman showed me a painting she did, with her father's voyeuristic eyes hanging on her body like suction cups).
- The perpetrator appears naked in front of the child (exhibitionism).
- The child is encouraged to walk around naked in the apartment or garden.
- The child is touched and kissed against his will.
- The child is asked to kiss and stroke the perpetrator.
- The perpetrator looks at pornographic pictures or watches pornographic films with the child.
- The perpetrator masturbates in front of the child, and asks her to masturbate him or to let him sexually arouse her and bring her to orgasm.
- The perpetrator (male or female) asks the child to suck his penis or lick her vagina.
- This leads to penetration of the child's mouth, anus, vagina with fingers or penis, even sometimes in babies.
- A boy is sexually stimulated or forced to have intercourse with his mother or sister.

Immediate reactions in the trauma situation

The feelings (pain, fear, disgust, anger, shame) that arise during sexual traumatisation are unbearable for the victim, and therefore must be split off. This causes numbness in certain areas or in the whole body. During the assaults the body freezes or it becomes limp and surrenders. Attempts are even made to psychologically leave the body, to escape in the imagination, e.g. behind a curtain, into a houseplant in the room or into a picture on the wall. The entire event is increasingly experienced by the child as unreal or as a bad dream. Detailed descriptions and case studies can be found, amongst others, in my books 'Trauma, Fear and Love' (2014, p. 123 ff.) and 'My Body, My Trauma, My I' (2018, p. 310 ff.).

A child's trauma survival strategies

Since the perpetrator is within the family or is a close relation, children remain in contact with the perpetrator, and it is even more urgent for the child to develop trauma survival strategies to endure this. I have already described some symptoms that are a result of sexual trauma, such as getting sick, wetting the bed, conspicuous behaviour at school or skipping school entirely. If one delves deeper into the layers of the child's psyche during therapy sessions, a number of inner parts become visible that are fixed at different ages and lead isolated existences. There are parts which

- are frozen in a state of trauma-feelings (fear, shame, disgust, pain),
- deny everything that has happened,
- do not want to remember anything,
- are angry at the perpetrator and would like to kill him,
- are angry at their own powerlessness and despise themselves for that,
- no longer trust anyone,
- feel completely worthless,
- blame themselves for everything,
- hang on to the perpetrator through their illusions of love ("My dad is the only person who loves me and cares for me."),
- identify completely with the perpetrator's needs and points of view,
- feel the perpetrator's shame as if it were their own,

- feel sexually aroused by the perpetrator,
- want to sexually satisfy the perpetrator and think that it is right to do so.

Since sexual trauma represents the third stage in a person's psychotrauma biography if it occurs within the family, the child's healthy 'I' and 'want' functions are already severely damaged. They have already been pushed into the background by the entangled family relationships. The child is already psychologically in a state of the trauma of love and has difficulty distinguishing between himself and his mother, father or siblings. He has largely had to take on the views of his parents: "Actually you are superfluous, but since you're already here, at least make yourself useful to us!" So the child may sense that his mother avoids the father's sexual interest and she is happy when the father sneaks up to the child's bed at night to satisfy himself sexually, and she gets a rest from him. Women may also deliberately place children between themselves and their partners in the marriage bed, so that the husband vents his frustrations against the child and not them.

The child's 'I' and 'want' are further negated by the sexual trauma, and so have no chance to develop healthily within his family. The splits in the child's psyche and in his or her whole organism become deeper and more numerous, so it is no surprise that in a sexually traumatised child there are self-destructive parts that may also think of suicide, plan it and will, on occasion, succeed in carrying it out. This can look like an accident to the outside world. Such children see no other way out of their hopeless situation. They cannot get away from their parents and they cannot get emotionally close to them. Help seldom comes from the outside either; often the child's perpetrator parents are even admired by other people around them – it is the child who has out of nothing suddenly turned out badly and unfortunately causes his poor parents all those problems.

Trauma of the whole bonding system

A sexual trauma is, from my point of view, a classic example of what I call a 'bonding system trauma'. The parents, who should be a safe haven for the child to develop in a healthy way physically and psychologically, instead drag the child into their psychotrauma biography and make them their victim. The child becomes hopelessly entangled in the already existing perpetrator-victim dynamics between his parents, between his siblings (if he has them) or between his parents and their parents.

- From the beginning of his life the child's natural willingness to love and trust unconditionally is betrayed.
- Rejection, neglect and aggression are presented to him as love by his parents.
- The generational boundaries become blurred because the child has to take care of the childish needs of his traumatised parents.
- A reversal of responsibility takes place, where the child becomes the 'adult' and is held responsible for what the grown-ups do to him.
- The child can never do right in such a family. Whatever he does, it is wrong.

It is no wonder that the child loses his original trust in his parents, siblings, close relatives, teachers and psychologists, and can no longer talk to anyone about what he is experiencing. The child increasingly sinks into the chaos of his fragmented inner parts. His sexual trauma leads to widespread confusion in all his psychological structures ('I', 'want', feelings, thinking, action). Thereby his future as a trauma perpetrator is mapped out.

That is why bonding system traumas inevitably continue over generations. In a traumatised bonding system, no one can develop a healthy psyche nor identity and work through their traumatisations. Nobody has a sense of or knows who they really are. The mother confuses herself with both her own mother and her child. The father sees his father in his own son and the son cannot clearly distinguish between his father and grandfather. In such bonding systems one can only be a victim or a perpetrator, alternating between the two and remaining trapped in victim and perpetrator attitudes. As a result, children are confused as to what belongs to them, and what belongs to their parents. They will likely feel within themselves the sexual traumatisation feelings that actually belong to their parents. The psychological structures of parents and children become blurred in such families, everything becomes confused and mothers and fathers cannot experience themselves as separate from their children.

Don't touch me!

> A mother told me: "Now I understand why my son is restless at night and says: 'Don't touch me!' That was my situation as a child when my grandfather came to my bed at night and touched me all over."

The vicious circle of sexual traumatisation

When sexually traumatised women become mothers themselves, it is highly likely that they will also traumatise their own children. Even the conception may be the result of an affair or something that is unwanted in the existing partnership, such as coercion, or even rape. Pregnancy and birth can then escalate into horror for the mother and the growing child. The bodily state that pregnancy entails means that the mother can no longer split off her physical sensations and feelings as she did before. During pregnancy, sexually traumatised women are often involved in violent relationship conflicts with their traumatised partners, and they may hardly notice the child in their belly. The child, then, has no chance of healthy contact with his mother and no possibility to avoid the body contact with her.

Because of the avalanche of hormones released in the mother, the birth process can also lead to a breakdown of her familiar splitting process, and as a result the doctors can be perceived as assaulting perpetrators, and midwives and nurses experienced like the mother's own mother, who, in childhood, stood by and watched but did not protect (Simkin and Klaus, 2015). The consequence of this may be an extremely prolonged and excruciating labour, because of the lack of cooperation between mother and child; or, on the other hand, a precipitate delivery, because the mother wants to get rid of the child, who triggers her trauma feelings, as quickly as possible.

After birth too, sexually traumatised mothers are often unable to allow their child to get physically close to them because this also triggers their trauma feelings. Nor is emotional closeness possible, because dulling their feelings has been the means by which they survived their own traumatisations. Inflammation of the mother's nipples can also be a symptom of trauma, so that the woman does not to have to breastfeed her child, and can avoid direct skin-to-skin contact. And so, for the child, the trauma of love follows its unrelenting course, especially if the child was not wanted. He has to stay quiet now and should only be there for whatever the mother wants from him.

Since a daughter's behaviour can act as a trigger and remind a mother unconsciously of her own helplessness and vulnerability, the mother may react repeatedly with rejection and anger towards her daughter. On the other hand, trauma triggers can lead to panic reactions, and to the daughter being forbidden to do anything. Whenever the child triggers the sexual trauma in her mother, all hell breaks loose: the mother fires up all her survival strategies, freaks out, becomes aggressive, and the child no longer has any chance of protecting herself. Such children learn to pay attention to their mother's subtle emotional shifts, constantly on the alert for a possible further outbreak of violence. With their hyper-alert antennae they become highly sensitive to everything that emanates from the mother. When they are near her, they have no possibility to feel themselves.

Therefore, the daughters of sexually traumatised mothers are in great danger of being the victims of sexual traumatisation themselves. They can easily be ensnared by a trauma perpetrator who will feed their illusion that he sees them, loves them and is there to serve them.

From the beginning, sons are a screen onto which their sexually traumatised mothers can project perpetrators, as the following example illustrates.

Offensive smell

"My son's smell reminded me of my father's and grandfather's smell. I could hardly stand it." This was the statement of a woman who had gradually become aware of the full extent of her sexual trauma in childhood. In the meantime, her older son had already sexually traumatised the younger son.

Sons can be perceived as threatening and dangerous even when in the womb. The male genitals can increasingly prove to be triggers as the son gets older. Sons become emotionally confused as a result, occasionally falling into psychotic states because they are in resonance with the trauma experiences of their mothers, and can no longer distinguish between their mother's feelings and their own.

I – man – wrong

I have observed in therapeutic processes how an unborn son has fought to suppress his male sex because he felt his mother's rejection of it. For him to be a man is highly threatening for his mother, and therefore wrong. So the child is not allowed to be male, and cannot become an adult man.

Even after birth, sexually traumatised mothers signal to their sons that they are only wanted if they do not threaten their mother with their sexuality, and on the contrary help the mother in her everyday life against evil men, e.g. the father. These sons then become well-behaved 'mummy's boys', who can anticipate every wish of their mothers.

In these ways, such sons become professional 'women whisperers' taking the side of women in general against men. Or more often they become the next generation of sexual trauma perpetrators. Some end up with prostitutes and especially with dominatrices, where they are able to re-enact that love is the same thing as experiencing pain and humiliation. 'Lust = pain = I am wrong': they know this from the very beginning of their lives in their relationship with their mother.

Identity-Oriented Psychotrauma Therapy (IoPt)

Why psychotherapy?

Everything that we do or do not do is linked to the state of our psyche. Our psyche is therefore the most important resource that we humans have at our disposal to enable us to lead a good life. How we live and how we live together with our fellow human beings depends on how well our psyche can adequately grasp the realities around us. Therefore our psyche needs careful attention, loving care and a regular update.

When we embark on the journey towards addressing our psyche, we must ask ourselves: How deep do we want to immerse ourselves? Is it enough to just swim on the surface and deal with the conflicts or symptoms we see there? Or do we want to dive deeper? Do we perhaps even want to descend to the very bottom of our psyche? Do we have the courage for that? Is there enough oxygen to get all the way down, or will we have to turn back halfway because we run out of air? In the meantime, do we have to come to the surface again to gather more strength in order to be able to get further down?

My own experience is that the deeper we dive into our psyche, the more experienced our therapist must be. If we want to see what lies at the bottom of our psyche, our therapist must show us the way, encourage us and give us the certainty that we will return to the surface safe and sound.

Early psychological damage often occurred during the time we were still in our mother's womb. That is why we had difficulties leaving the womb with our psyche in one piece during the birth process. Unbearable loneliness tortured us when we were still very small and helpless. Physical and psychological wounds were inflicted on us by the people we loved most as children: by our mother and our father.

Our therapeutic companion must not be scared off by taboos about revealing the truth. Medical or psychological experts can do their best to try and make our symptoms disappear for a short time. However, when it comes to their underlying traumatic causes, we have to take responsibility ourselves, and we must clearly want to do so. Because we take ourselves seriously and are important to ourselves. Because we want more than just survival. Because we want to lead a good life.

If we ignore our psyche, we ignore ourselves. Unfortunately, this is still happening worldwide on a huge scale. Hardly anyone has a clue when it comes to their own psyche and how it is functioning, and very few people try to understand it in depth. In most societies the view still prevails that psychological disorders indicate metabolic problems in the brain. And if it is confessed that psychotherapy is needed at all, it is only for severely disturbed people. Young people will happily call each other a 'psycho' as a term of abuse. Instead of offering assistance to those with emotional problems, the general response is to provide chemical and moral crutches. Therefore, it seems to many that it is something to be ashamed of if they do end up seeking therapeutic help, or if they have to admit to being traumatised. Many people tend to go secretly to a psychotherapist and rarely reveal this to those around them.

But in fact, in my experience, it's really the other way around. It is a very clear sign of mental health when someone takes responsibility for and deals with his or her own psyche, and asks for professional help. In doing this, a person takes genuine care of him or herself, and takes responsibility for their own life. She starts a good process in order not to constantly expect her environment and her fellow human beings to accept her many psychotrauma survival strategies. Imagine how different societies would look if all those who today do a lot of harm to the rest of humanity within their families and administrative, economic or political leadership positions, started by cleaning up the chaos in their own psyche first instead of unconsciously directing their unresolved trauma feelings outwards and onto others!

Identity-Oriented Psychotrauma Thereapy (IoPT)

I find it a very responsible act for mothers and fathers to wake up and arrange therapeutic help for themselves when they discover that they have been burdening their children with the weight of their own psychotraumas for a long time. This may be a painful realisation, but it is better to set out on the path of change late rather than not at all. It would be particularly wise, of course, if men and women were to put their psyches in order *before* they become parents. Some at least already do this (Vasile, 2018).

What's the point of trauma?

Faced with terrible blows at the hands of fate, many people wonder what the meaning of it is. I recently received the following enquiry by e-mail: "The question of the meaning and purpose of trauma also arises because there can be no individual who has not suffered trauma. Therefore, in my opinion, a trauma MUST have a point."

If instead of talking about 'fate' or 'good' and 'bad' people, we use the expression 'psychotrauma' as a form of explanation, we can say that the point of trauma can be a personal or collective wake-up call. Only then can we ask ourselves how such psychotraumas can be prevented in the future. We must first identify the causes of the respective psychotraumas.

Early childhood psychotraumas can be reduced in their frequency if parents are willing and able, in their healthy psychological parts, to want, love and protect their children. This would also reduce the frequency of sexual trauma because fewer people would grow up with sexuality that cannot develop properly, and so would not then become sexual trauma perpetrators against other people, or be exploited as sexual trauma victims by others. Children who are not traumatised are much more able to develop cooperative forms of relationships and refrain from violent solutions. World peace ultimately starts in the womb of our mother and in the way we are brought up. From the foundation of a healthy psyche, we humans can self-responsibly influence our path in life and our physical and psychological well-being.

If, on the other hand, psychotraumas are denied and pushed into the unconscious, our trauma survival strategies will continue to do senseless things, still trying to prevent something that has long since already happened. Instead of identifying the causes and healing the psychological wounds, we continually fight with the consequences of our traumas. In this way, the chaos in our psyche becomes even greater, and we cause more chaos in the world around us. Through our trauma survival strategies we continue to destroy our life force and that of other people. If, on the other hand, we understand the messages contained within our symptoms, which are caused by trauma, we can find our way back to a healthy kind of life force, both as individuals and as a human community.

Since early psychotraumas are not accessible by our own consciousness, psychotherapeutic support is necessary for the recognition and treatment of them. We can only be partially successful if we try to do the therapy on our own.

IoPT as a Method of Psychotherapy

Preliminary remarks

Over the last 25 years I have gradually developed a form of psychotherapy that is capable of bringing traumatisations of the human psyche into consciousness, and of supporting steps towards the reintegration of the split identity. I call this method of psychotherapy Identity-Oriented Psychotrauma Therapy (IoPT).

In my opinion, each individual form of psychotherapy has four main components:

- Theory,
- Method,
- Technique,
- The person who is the therapeutic companion.

Identity-Oriented Psychotrauma Thereapy (IoPT)

I have presented the theoretical background knowledge for IoPT in nine books so far. This book complements the previous books, and updates them with further reflections and information on human sexuality and sexual psychotraumas.

I have been confronted with thousands of cases of sexual traumatisation in my practice in Munich and in my seminars worldwide. Based on a wealth of growing understanding, I have developed a therapy method that is able to get to the causes of the many physical and psychological symptoms, and that focuses on the promotion of a healthy human identity. It therefore systematically supports the development of the healthy 'I' and 'want' of the people who entrust themselves to therapeutic support. For the practice and quality of a method of psychotherapy, the extent of the identity development in the therapist himself is crucial. Which of his psychotraumas has he been able to work on, and which ones has he not yet explored? Here again is an example from my own experience.

My twin-trauma

I realised this when, better late than never, I was able to integrate my own trauma of a lost twin. Only from that point on could I start to recognise the prenatal twin dynamics in the self-encounters of others I was accompanying therapeutically, and support their resolution in a targeted way.

The Intention Method

I call the method that forms the basis of Identity-oriented Psychotrauma Therapy (IoPT) the 'Intention Method'. Its purpose is to make redundant the splits in the human psyche that have been caused as a result of trauma. The main components of a healthy identity that have been pushed into the background must be restored to their original role: the healthy 'I' and our own 'want', so that our own feelings, thoughts and actions are appropriate to reality, and our identifications with the psyches of other people dissolve. The Intention Method should:

- give access to the person's psyche,
- show internal and external realities as they really are,
- bring unconscious structures to light,
- make trauma-induced splits visible,
- be oriented towards the causes and not the symptoms,
- involve the body,
- support the expression of feelings,
- enable us to overcome our splits.

The point is to understand our own psyche better: How is it constructed? How does it develop? How does it react to trauma? Our psyche should not be an impenetrable mystery to us, but something that follows clear laws and cause-and-effect relations and therefore can be understood and influenced.

The therapy method must reveal the internal and external reality as it actually is, and not as the person concerned (or maybe even the therapist) might wish it to be. Illusory ideas, desires, affirmations or beliefs must be open to be questioned and seen for what they really are.

Through the method the difference between healthy psychological parts and trauma survival strategies should become clear. With the help of the Intention Method I learned to identify trauma-surviving strategies as follows:

- They sometimes act on a belief that their intentions and goals are the way to healing, while in reality they are the way to further physical and psychological self-destruction.
- Psychotrauma survival strategies re-stage the old traumas and continually generate new ones.
- If we are feeling bad our survival strategies can claim that the uncovering of the traumatising past is to blame.
- Even in a therapy process they may appease and gloss over the reality.
- They will tell terrible stories of what happened in their lives but without any feelings.
- They will use all the tools at their disposal to avoid feeling.
- They leap into action, trying to console, appease and

distract when they come into contact with the reality of traumatised parts.
- They are deeply loyal to the perpetrators.

To be someone who can accompany someone else in a useful therapeutic way, it is supremely important to have a good understanding of the various forms of psychotrauma survival strategies. Then it becomes clear that in the therapy process a survival 'I' must first transform into a healthy 'I', so that in a later process the basis is available for enabling access to the split-off traumatised parts. Body and psyche must be able to be experienced again as a whole entity. In the end, one's own biography should not only be a collection of fragmentary episodes, but a clear timeline of our life.

The Intention

In order for the person with whom I am working therapeutically to stand in the centre and take responsibility for his healing process, it is up to him to formulate what he wants to look at in his therapy sessions. What moves him? What does he want to deal with? Which of his issues, questions or problems does he want to actively deal with here and now? I summarise all this with the term the 'Intention'.

At the beginning of each therapy process, I ask the person concerned to formulate their intention without any preliminary discussion. The chosen intention can be a whole sentence as a statement or a question (e.g. 'Was I sexually traumatised?'). The punctuation marks can also be one of the elements that will be represented in the process, and provide information. It can also be single words (e.g. 'I Fear Men') or a combination of words and drawings. It is also possible to combine individual word groups, which can be useful when working with people who have a mother tongue other than that of the group or the therapist for example (see Figure 9). I call the person who has the intention the 'Intention Holder'.

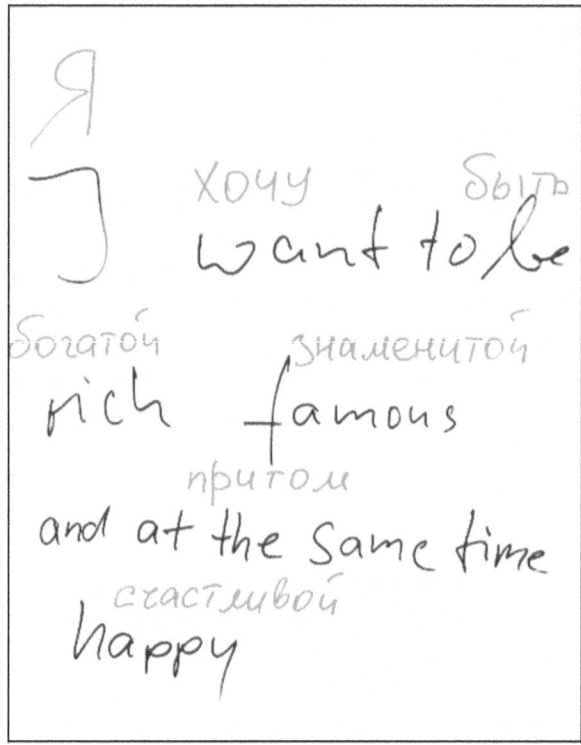

Figure 9: An example of an Intention with partially combined parts of the Intention. The mother tongue of this Intention Holder was Russian: "I want to be rich, famous and at the same time happy".

I want to be ...

In this case, it turned out that one part ('at the same time') indicated a sexual traumatisation, which at this time the Intention Holder was not able to see because she was still trapped in the trauma of love, and so still in illusions of love in relation to her parents who were represented by the elements 'rich' (father) and 'happy' (mother).

Identity-Oriented Psychotrauma Thereapy (IoPT)

It is part of the nature of the Intention Method that I give the Intention Holders no guidelines regarding the content of their intention – what they should look at in their therapy session. I always trust that what they choose will be the right thing for them at this time. For this Intention Method approach, I do not need any background stories or reports about what has already happened or what they have already dealt with. In order to accompany a person therapeutically all I need is an Intention formulated by the person concerned that he has come up with himself.

Meanwhile, out of my many experiences over the last years, the Intention should not contain more than five elements in order not to bring too much out of the unconscious into the light all at once, because this can ask too much of all those involved. In addition, my experience has shown that the more elements an Intention has, the more trauma survival strategies it contains, so I emphasise to the Intention Holder that the number five represents the maximum we can work with, and that Intentions with less than five information units can be very productive. I have reduced the number of elements from seven to five whilst writing this book, so the example above took place when the person was still able to choose seven resonators for her intention.

Talking in order not to feel the pain

We have to take refuge in splitting during traumatic situations because we cannot withstand our feelings, the fear of death, the physical and psychological pain, the shame, disgust and impotent rage, the destructive potential of which we are so frightened.

Years of working with the Intention Method have shown that the integration of splits works best when someone is ready to feel the split-off pain. This releases him from the entanglement with his perpetrators, frees him from their power over him and brings him back in touch with himself and the present. There are two distinct forms of pain involved:

1. The pain of not being wanted and not being loved. These refer to the mother and/or the father, and signal the persistent desire to finally be seen and loved by him/her. This pain and the tears shed over it are endless since they originate from the victim attitude survival strategy of the small child, who continues to cling to the perpetrator.
2. The pain over the lost contact with oneself. This pain is very deep, but has a goal that is achievable. In this way, it is also finite. Contact with ourselves can be re-established when the pain that arose during the original split is felt. These pains are short and intense. In the long run they lead to deep inner peace and contentment.

To feel these split-off deep pains, however, is something that the person in their survival 'I' fears and so thwarts with all their strength. They often also do not know the difference between the qualities of these pains. They prefer to talk constantly, to know and analyse everything in detail, to tell the same stories over and over again in order not to have to feel at all. They are afraid that the feelings coming to the surface are fatal, annihilating and destructive, and will lead to madness or suicide – which would have been the case in the original trauma situation of course: for example, if, as a child, you were threatened with more beatings if you did not stop crying immediately. Therefore there is a tendency for the survival parts of a person to want to use the offered framework and the therapy time for these discussions in order to confirm their importance and indispensability, and to keep control.

I have therefore, in the time in which I developed the Intention Method, made changes to it repeatedly, primarily in an effort to limit as far as possible the survival strategies of talking away the feelings and fleeing into 'doing' instead feeling. The healthy parts need to be given enough space to be there and develop so as to retrieve the split-off traumatised parts from their exile. I know from my own experience how much trauma can have accumulated in a lifetime.

Identity-Oriented Psychotrauma Thereapy (IoPT)

Too much pain

Over the course of one week, I did two processes, taking a closer look at myself with these two intentions: 'I want to feel my split-off pain' and 'Why do I have tinnitus?' This made it clear to me how multi-layered my trauma pains are. I had to split all of these pains off:

- *The never-ending pain about a twin who died next to me in the womb because both of us were not wanted by our mother.*
- *The violent headaches that were a result of a birth process that went on for too long.*
- *The pain from the very beginning of not being seen and loved by my mother.*
- *The physical pain in my throat and head because my father had, in a violent rage, shaken and beaten me because of my screaming as a baby.*
- *The pain that my mother didn't protect me.*
- *The pain of being breastfed for only a few weeks and then almost starving and becoming dehydrated because of a milk powder that I was intolerant to.*
- *The pain of my childhood loneliness and my retreat into isolation.*
- *The pain of my blocked 'want' that does not know whether to be full of love or destructive.*
- *Physical pain that I have inflicted on myself out of a lack of caring for myself.*
- *The pain of burying myself in my work and escaping into merely functioning.*
- *The pain of not recognising myself, of confusing myself with the perpetrators, of not trusting myself and therefore of attacking myself.*

In these two self-encounters it became clear to me that it was impossible to let all these pains and fears come up in me and feel them all at once. It would only be possible in smaller doses. I therefore need to be patient with myself.

The practical way of working with the Intention Method

First of all, the Intention Holder writes up his Intention on a whiteboard. The individual parts (the words, elements that make up the intention) are then written down again on smaller pieces of paper, which are stuck on to nametags. In a group setting, these badges are then distributed to members of the group, as they are asked to resonate with the respective word or symbol. In this respect I speak here of a 'resonance technique', and I call the people who resonate with the parts of the intention resonators.

Resonance is the basic principle of psychological self-development and transformation (Bauer, 2019). Carl Rogers saw 'mirroring' as the most effective means available to a psychotherapist and counsellor to bring his clients into a process of self-exploration. To do this, it is necessary to resonate empathically with the clients (Rogers, 1992). The Intention Method I developed allows the Intention Holder, by use of floor markers in an Individual session and the group members in a group session, to go into resonant vibration with his psychological structures. When this happens he often feels deeply understood, can trust himself and can dare to change. This is why I do not call these processes 'constellations', a technical term that comes from the tradition of family constellations, but prefer to call them 'self-encounters' in order to define this specific form of therapy.

The Stance of the Therapist

The main goal of Identity-Oriented Psychotrauma Therapy (IoPT) is to find our way back to our own identity. Since identity, in my opinion, is a fact that goes beyond attachment and relationship, we do not feel dependent on any relationship as long as we are not traumatised. Nor do we feel dependent on our relationship with our mother, even if it is existentially necessary for our initial development.

It is not necessarily the case that our relationship with our mother is problematic. It is only when our mother does not want us as her child or cannot be there for us emotionally because of her own traumatisations, that it becomes so. In this case we have to split off from ourselves and feel dependent on her. We then remain dependent on relationships as adults, because we actually psychologically remain in the child state of survival that needs to bond (the trauma of love).

This state of dependency is also transferred onto us as therapists, and it all depends on whether we accept this offer of transference and enter into a potentially entangled relationship with the respective person, or whether we do not accept this offer and instead always redirect the person back to himself. This happens sometimes during a self-encounter; so for example, if the Intention Holder turns to me seeking help, I consistently refer him back to those resonating with his psychological parts. For him, this may initially be experienced as a rejection, or even as a lack of professional competence, but ultimately it serves to promote the healthy development of his 'I' rather than any dependence on me. This also relieves me as a therapist, because the person bringing the intention and the resonators feel what is going on for him, and I do not have to. I also do not impose on the Intention Holder anything that might have to do with me, or anything that I believe might be going on for him now, even anything that might be based on my many years of therapeutic experience. As a therapeutic companion you can still often be wrong. By referring the person's attention back to the resonators, you are exploiting to the full the potential of the resonators, and do not place yourself, as the therapist, above them or feel superior to them. For me, IoPT therapy means: I organise, open and hold the space for the self-healing powers of the psyche of the person concerned. It is not up to me how much happens in a self-encounter, but up to the Intention Holder. If I think it makes sense, I can bring in representitives of impulses from outside. However, I always first ask the Intention Holder if he wants to hear something from me. This is important because the journey back to our own 'I' cannot happen through a relationship with someone else, i.e. through a new dependence on a therapist. Such a dependence will cause the person to get further stuck in his trauma of love, meaning that he cannot come close to his trauma of identity. I am convinced that the trauma of identity is the root of all further complications in a person's trauma biography.

For the therapeutic accompaniment of such processes one thing is needed above all: patient waiting until self-resonance happens. Nothing should be imposed on the Intention Holder, however plausible it may seem in individual cases, otherwise we will be back to what the Intention Holder experienced in his own childhood, where something is attributed to him that is not his own truth, and therefore is not his own true identity. If, during the process, the Intention Holder does not come into an emotional resonance for a long time, then the therapist must not be tempted to try to force this. It is important as a therapeutic companion to internalise the principle that healing is always self-healing. It can only be stimulated from the outside (e.g. by asking questions, or suggesting certain sentences, that reveal realities), so that a self-healing resonance is sparked on the inside. Then, in an Intention Process, the therapist can wait calmly and persistently for the moment when the expressions of those who are resonating begin to vibrate with a suppressed emotion in the Intention Holder, and this accumulated energy is then discharged. In this moment a part of the healing of the split takes place, and is often a joy for me to witness.

Group Therapy

In a group therapy situation, when the Intention Holder is ready and indicates that the process can start, those people selected go into resonance with a word or sign from the intention. They can do this by following their experience, initially without talking. After about one to two minutes, this non-verbal phase can be stopped because the resonance happens spontaneously and intuitively. It quickly becomes clear to each person resonating what his or her respective part of the Intention is about.

Then the Intention Holder goes around to each of the resonators, in whatever order he chooses, and exchanges experiences with them whilst they are in resonance. According to my trauma model, healthy, traumatised and survival parts emerge and make the psychological structure of the intention tangible. Through his or her own resonance with the parts of the intention, a process of change occurs in the Intention Holder on an emotional and cognitive level, and will also include physical reactions. The depth of the emotional processes for which the Intention Holder is open depends on the Intention and his willingness.

This procedure and the expert guidance of an IoPT therapist ensure that there is no uncontrolled retraumatisation during the self-encounter.

Individual therapy

In an individual therapy session, the notes with the individual parts of Intention are attached to floor markers, which are designated as either female or male, and a "V" cut into the marker indicates the direction in which the respective part is looking. In my practice these floor markers are comprised of eight different colours and three different sizes. When the Intention Holder intuitively selects the markers and lays them out on the floor, he has his whole Intention before him as a starting picture.

Then the Intention Holder stands on the floor markers in whichever order he chooses. In this way, profound changes can take place and psychological splits can be overcome.

Sexual Inhibition

A 50-year-old man had the following intention (Figure 10):

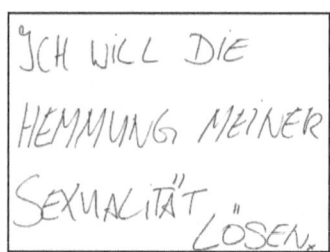

I (ICH) WANT (WILL) to release (LÖSEN) THE (DIE) INHIBITION (HEMMUNG) of my (MEINER) SEXUALITY (SEXUALITÄT).

Using the floor markers, the man laid out the following initial picture (see Figure 11).
INHIBITION (HEMMUNG), THE (DIE) und SEXUALITY (SEXUALITÄT) were represented with round, female floor markers. For the 'I' (ICH) he had chosen a male marker and the colour black. All the floor markers were pointing in the same direction. Initially the man stood on INHIBITION and felt sadness. I asked

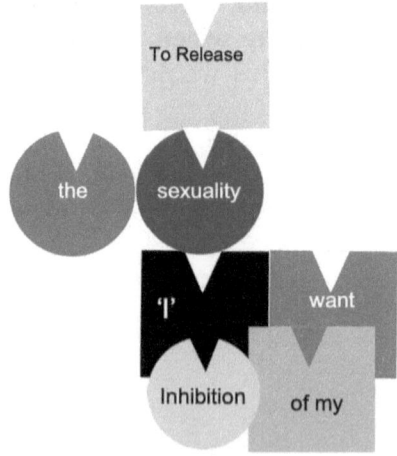

Figure 11: The Intention at the start of the process as represented by floor markers.

him what age he felt he was as INHIBITION and he said between 10 and 12 – before the onset of puberty. He did not notice that he was on a female floor marker. Only when I drew his attention to it did it become clear to him. He told me that during this time he was still sharing the bedroom with his mother, and that she had once seen him with his erect penis sticking up under his blanket, and she turned him onto his side in disgust.

He then stood on his 'I', and was repelled by the black colour. He did not like himself. He now saw that he liked the violet colour of SEXUALITY, that was in front of him, but now he recognised that this also was a female floor marker, so it was not his sexuality. He then stood on WANT, and he quickly took the SEXUALITY name tag off the female marker and put it on the 'I'.

In the process, he discovered that THE represented his mother, and he felt that the INHIBITION had originally come from her, who he said was disgusted by harmless love scenes on TV. As a child and adolescent, he had to adapt to her sexual inhibitions and identify with them. Accordingly he was ignorant and shy when it came to his first contact with girls.

It also became clear to him that he was taking this inhibition pattern that developed in his relationship with his mother (who had unintentionally become pregnant with him and had raised him as a single parent), and was now transferring this into his present relationship with his partner.

Eventually the following final picture came, with which he was very satisfied (see Figure 12). His own parts and those of his mother were now separated, and he could also accept the black colour of his 'I' because his childhood and youth situation with his mother had made him both angry and sad. He no longer condemned himself for this.

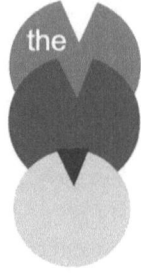

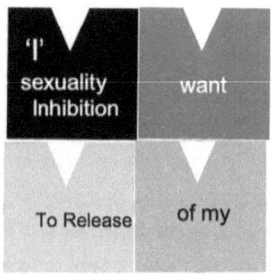

Figure 12: The final picture of the individual session.

Resolving our trauma biography from the roots up

When I started working as a therapist I thought that sexual traumatisation was the worst thing that could happen to a person. Today I know that these seductive and violent transgressions of boundaries, especially when these traumatisations happen within the family, are just the logical and consequential continuation and intensification of the trauma of identity and the trauma of love. If there is a trauma of love, it means that a child's primal need for physical contact, to be seen and loved by the mother, is not fulfilled, and the child is then open to every hint of affection or physical closeness from others. Consequently he turns longingly to a father who may only give him scant attention, or who may from time to time tenderly stroke his head and call him nice names, but in return may demand sexual satisfaction. Because the perpetrator offers the child physical contact and pretends to love him, the child in his need for attention and love easily falls for it, and endures the sexual assaults and splits them

Identity-Oriented Psychotrauma Thereapy (IoPT)

off. The more often this happens, the more normal it seems to the victim of a sexual trauma.

In addition, these children may have to endure these sexual acts from their father, grandfather, or the mother's boyfriend because their mother, who has often suffered a sexual trauma as a child herself, wants to be relieved of the sexual advances of the men near her. Because these mothers have a blind spot to their own sexual trauma, they are blind to what the perpetrators do right before their eyes to their child. They also tend to choose male partners who unconsciously remind them of their childhood perpetrators.

For the child, sexual trauma takes place when there is already a state of a trauma of love and a trauma of identity. It can even serve as a trauma survival strategy for the trauma of identity and love. So, because sexual psychotrauma is embedded in the psychotrauma biography, it makes no sense therapeutically to address a sexual childhood trauma directly. Until the victim has addressed his trauma of identity and trauma of love he is still too little in contact with his healthy 'I', and too entangled in his love illusions with the perpetrator and any complicit perpetrators.

Normally, the first thing that comes into focus in a therapy session is the entangled bond with the mother. This must be recognised and understood. The split child has survival parts that cling to the traumatised and traumatising mother with a tenacity and perseverance that no one would believe unless they saw it themselves in a therapy process. This is why I prefer to work in groups, because the group participants learn from each other and can observe what happens in their traumatised psyche from a more distanced perspective. Even if the mother has been dead for a long time, for example, the symbiotically entangled child parts in the psyche of a person continue to exist for as long as that person does not work purposefully and deliberately on the resolution of his psychotrauma biography.

The trauma of love often plays out in our present-day lives. Many mothers come for therapy because they want to help their children who are displaying highly conspicuous symptoms, or because they are stuck in a futile fight with, from their point of view, 'narcissistic' partners. It is important to make them aware that this conflict is a trauma survival strategy within the framework of generations of continual perpetrator-victim dynamics within their families. Only in this way can they recognise how pointless such battles and such offers of help are. That is why I decided a long time ago not to write court reports in such disputes, even though I am often asked about them.

Those who are caught up in a perpetrator-victim dynamic must first learn that they cannot save another person from their trauma. The only sensible thing anyone can do in his therapy, is to look at himself and his own psychotrauma biography. The path to ourselves is the only realistic basis for gradually transforming relationships with our children or partners into a constructive way of living together, or at least coexistence. To look at the suffering and pain of others is a distraction from our own pain. When parents can finally say 'yes' to themselves, their children are freed from their entanglements with the parents.

The desire for maternal and paternal love and the pain of not having been loved by our mother and father must be expressed in therapy. In the end, a person can only come out of the trauma of love if they can get in touch with their trauma of identity and allow the pain, sadness, fear and anger of not having been wanted as a child. The pain of not having been loved usually masks this primal pain of having to split from ourselves. Only when we feel this pain, can our own 'yes', which is there at the beginning of every person's life, be freed from the devastating 'no' of our mother or urges. Only then can we understand that the idea of having been a 'wanted child' meant nothing more or less than being totally at the service of our mother's or father's illusions and trauma survival urges. Only in this way can our own 'want' become free from wanting to be like our own mother or father. Instead of continuing to long for our mother, it is imperative to develop a longing for ourselves.

Identity-Oriented Psychotrauma Thereapy (IoPT)

Finding connection to our healthy 'I'

Meaningful psychotherapy would not be possible if, despite all the accumulated trauma experiences in a person's biography, there were not still healthy psychological components available. Fortunately, as far as I can see from all the therapy processes I have accompanied so far, this is true. Even in the worst cases of ritual violence it is possible to rebuild healthy psychological structures, because the basic principle of our human psyche is to make reality accessible to us as it actually is. As long as we are alive and want to become whole, many things are possible. If we are ready to face our pain, then some events may even happen, which we would otherwise only dismiss as a coincidence, as the following example illustrates.

Self-encounter with a fruit fly

Cornelia had to experience the whole burden of a trauma biography in her childhood. She was not wanted, her parents tried to abort her, she did not get any love from her father or mother, both her father and her brother raped her, and so on. Her Intention for this piece of work was "I WANT TO FEEL."

Immediately TO FEEL jumped into the middle of the room like a little girl who was happy and looking for a playmate. However, WANT could not accept this offer. The person resonating with WANT struggled not to cry, suppressed her tears and stayed seated in her chair. The FULL-STOP hid behind his chair and remained there in a curled-up position. Cornelia went to the 'I', who had also remained frozen on her chair. In the role, the 'I' was not able to move or speak. However the resonator for 'I' came out of role and reported her experiences. She was still very small; her hands seemed to be just beginning to grow. She felt like she was frozen in amber. I, as the therapist, suggested to her that this might be the condition she found herself in after an abortion attempt by her mother, and encouraged Cornelia to realise this and let the pain associated with it come up in her. The more she succeeded and the more she could resist her impulses to want to help the 'I', the more alive the 'I' became. The resonator now slid from her chair onto the floor. After a while she discovered a small fruit fly on the carpet. She took the sheet of paper on which 'I' was written, and let the fruit fly crawl up on to it. Cornelia stayed in her sobbing and her pain and her 'I' devotedly took care of this little fruit fly and showed it to Cornelia. Cornelia took the paper with the fruit fly crawling on the edge. The fly stayed there when we had finished the work and all the resonators had been released from their roles. Cornelia then went to the roof terrace of my practice and let the fly out into the open air.

Without our own 'I', in other words without having a point of reference within ourselves, basically everything we do in our lives is pointless. Why should we make friends, form partnerships, have children, develop ourselves professionally, etc., when this has nothing to do with ourselves? Therefore it is the main purpose of the therapeutic endeavour of IoPT that the Intention Holder finds their way to themselves, rediscovers their own 'I' and is in permanent good contact with themselves. In the process of becoming 'I', our needs for closeness and security (symbiosis) as well as our needs for independence and freedom (autonomy) come down to a common point: when I love myself, when I compassionately embrace my split-off traumatised child parts, then I am free and independent; then I no longer have to struggle with how to distinguish myself from others who are not good for me. I am no longer at risk of being seduced because of my fear of loneliness, and I don't have to betray myself for the sake of supposed closeness, or deliver myself into the hands of a perpetrator just to avoid feeling alone.

As we gradually lay the foundations for a healthy identity, in other words if we gain a stable 'I' and our own 'want', then our sexual traumatisation can also be tackled step by step. There is often no awareness of the sexual trauma. In most cases, those affected cannot even imagine that 'something like this' could have happened to them, especially at the hands of a father or grandfather, whom they absolutely had idolised as a child and until today still do. The absence of any conscious memory is understandable when the sexual traumatisation happened in infancy, because we generally find it difficult to have conscious pictorial memories. But why do older children and even teenagers have no conscious memories of the sexual violence they had experienced, even when the violence has often taken place over many years? Here, the repression mechanism, the reality shredder of our psyche, does a thorough job, keeping the memories out of our consciousness until we are ready and resourced enough to face them.

Therefore, in my therapy groups it is often the case that a sexual trauma may surface as an aspect of someone's Intention. The person concerned first has to entertain the idea that there really could be something that he has completely split off from his memory to this current day. Usually it takes confirmation through further work on the matter of a sexual trauma for someone to get past his until now practiced survival strategies, and especially the forced abandonment of his own 'I', to get ready to acknowledge the fact of sexual traumatisation. In addition I often see that it is easier to consider neighbours, teachers, grandfathers, stepfathers or uncles as the likely sex trauma perpetrators rather than thinking it may be our own father or mother. Sometimes then the sexual trauma within an Intention does not appear just 'by accident', but the Intention Holder specifically seeks to deal with this topic, and formulates a focused Intention like this: "What was my experience of sexual trauma?" In the following example, sexual psychotrauma came to light without the Intention Holder consciously seeking for it.

Seduction?

"I WANT TO FEEL MYSELF!"
This was Michael's intention, after having done a very important piece of work for himself a month before, in which he was shown the full extent of his entanglement with his mother, his biological father and his adoptive father. With his new Intention, his 'I' was frozen and programmed to be obedient. His WANT was sprawled on a chair without any wanting at all, and would have preferred

> *not to be there. TO FEEL stood to one side and initially felt nothing. The resonator for MYSELF immediately jumped up and ran to the open window to gasp for air. The EXCLAMATION MARK danced around Michael from the beginning like a prima ballerina.*
>
> Michael now spoke of how his adoptive father had begun to sexually traumatise him from the age of six. Michael had to satisfy him orally. His adoptive father ensnared him with the promise that if Michael was willing to satisfy him, he would no longer hit Michael, which otherwise he would have to do because of Michael's misdeeds (for example spitting a piece of sausage out onto the wall). From then on Michael had 'asthma attacks'. He said he had got these attacks under control over the course of his life, but whenever a sexual conflict arose for him in his life, these suffocating attacks were there again. The emergence of the part of him that had difficulty breathing helped Michael admit emotionally that he had actually suffered a sexual trauma in his childhood.

People often protect themselves from becoming aware of their sexual traumas with the argument: "I have no memories whatsoever." But this is a trauma survival strategy that does not distinguish between conscious, visual memories and unconscious body memories. Not having pictorial memories of sexual trauma is a normal protective mechanism of our psyche. The visual memories of a sexual trauma only gradually emerge when we are able to cope with them emotionally.

Another argument often put forward against the possibility of having our own sexual trauma is that we could be entangled with our mother's sexual trauma. This cannot be completely dismissed, because as long as the person does not have stable contact with his healthy 'I', he is unable to distinguish his own feelings from those of others. Therefore, the therapeutic companion must keep an eye on this possibility if the topic of sexual trauma appears in a piece of Intention work. It must be clear from the overall context whether someone has suffered a sexual trauma himself, or whether the sexual trauma feelings of

Identity-Oriented Psychotrauma Thereapy (IoPT)

his mother have been superimposed upon him. As a rule, both are often the truth: the mother was sexually traumatised herself, and therefore could not prevent her child from becoming a victim of sexual trauma as well.

When sexual trauma makes itself apparent in a piece of work, it also usually reveals how strong the loyalty to the perpetrator still is, because it was often the perpetrator who gave the child that little bit more physical contact, attention and care than the mother, who was more often than not ice-cold and blocked by her own psychotrauma. Therefore, there is a great inner defensive struggle to let go of this substitute 'mother' figure, which the (usually male) perpetrator often represents for the child. It is difficult for many sexually traumatised people to bear the fact that this person also proves to be a formidable love illusion, so they hold on to this illusion of love as long as possible.

Bearing the shame

Another obstacle in the process of psychologically coping with our sexual trauma is the massive feelings of shame. For those affected, these feelings can be almost immeasurable. Typically in a group setting, it can be a big hurdle to reveal ourselves as someone who has experienced such disgusting things, and as someone who may have been involved in the perpetrator's games for many years, and has let himself be talked into doing disgusting acts as if it was something enjoyable. Therefore, in the face of all our feelings of shame, it is a big step forward to accept our own sexual victimhood as a fact. It takes a developed healthy 'I' and a determined 'want' of our own to utilise the potential of support offered by a therapy group. On the other hand it is tremendously beneficial and powerful when facts and truths are spoken in front of a group. This is even more supportive than when the witness is only a single therapist. The following example from a group seminar touched me deeply.

Rape

In a seminar, Marianne formulated this Intention: I WANT TO PROTECT MYSELF!

Straight away her 'I' is in a panic and wants to run away. When Marianne wants to go over to the EXCLAMATION MARK, for which she has chosen a man to resonate, the representative for 'MYSELF' loudly intervenes. 'MYSELF' is full of rage and fantasies of murder, she talks of stabbing and killing. Gradually Marianne remembers that at the age of 21 she had been locked up in a room on a horse farm by a horse owner who had earned her trust. When she refused to satisfy this man sexually, he grabbed scissors and held them to her neck. MYSELF is still stuck in this moment of time. She does not know if she is about to be killed or if she will kill someone else.

This is also a typical characteristic of rape. The victim splits off a part within herself that remains in its state of development before the act of violence took place. This part, which is in mortal danger, is caught up in the thought of what it would have had to do in order to get out of this life-threatening situation: in this case, to stab the man who holds the scissors to her throat.

The more Marianne talks about what happened to her in that situation, the more the resonator for MYSELF calms down. MYSELF listens to Marianne as she talks, and when she can finally say that she could not protect herself and that this man had actually raped her, MYSELF can then take Marianne in her arms and comfort her while she is feeling her pain. Marianne then cried long and hard.

It was also revealing in this process that MYSELF felt that Marianne had let her down several times after this rape. One occasion was during the trial in which Marianne did not, and could not, testify in front of the public on the witness stand as to what had happened to her. Marianne's case is a sad example of how sexual trauma victims are retraumatised by court trials, by judges and lawyers who are insensitive to psychotraumas. The victims have to split even further and get into even deeper internal conflicts. At the end of the trial, all Marianne was left with was a *profound fear of being convicted herself for bringing a false accusation.*

Furthermore, Marianne's case shows that rape in adolescence or adulthood is often the continuation of sexual traumatisation in childhood. Marianne had also experienced sexual trauma from her alcoholic father. Like the judge in the court trial, her mother had not believed her as to what her father had done to her, and had portrayed her as a liar in front of her neighbours.

Where to go with our rage?

If feelings of anger come up in an IoPT session, and are acted out by the Intention Holder, or by someone resonating in the process, this may feel like a rewarding experience for them. However, it can always be seen that such outbursts of aggression panic the younger internal parts of the Intention Holder, and these parts become afraid of the angry parts. The younger parts are not able to distinguish between the violence of the perpetrator and the reactive violence of the victim, and the abreaction of anger and expression of revenge fantasies therefore will deepen the existing splits. Both of these are ways of avoiding feeling the intense pain of having been made a victim of sexual violence, when, in fact, feeling the pain is what is necessary to dissolve the splits.

However, it can also be an important experience in the overall course of therapy to express our own anger without this leading to the annihilation of another person, or to our own self-destruction. In this way the 'I' can learn that it is possible here and now to express anger and then to calm down again and perhaps even laugh about one's own outburst of rage.

How to build up trust?

In these critical phases of the therapy process, when it comes to getting closer to the extremely painful and shameful event of sexual traumatisation, trust in the therapist is essential, especially since any form of closeness to another person can be experienced as threatening. The transference of the mother and father onto a male or female therapist inevitably takes place in psychotherapy; male therapists are then easily confused with the perpetrator, who at the time was also seen as the supposed saviour. Because of this, the feeling of dependence must *not* be encouraged by the therapist, because this reinforces the long-standing fears of being committed to someone again, and ultimately having to 'pay' for his help with sexual favours.

For us therapists, this means neither falling into the rescue trap ("Only I can save you from your misery!"), nor entering into a perpetrator-victim dialogue if we are wrongly attacked and accused. With a clear view of the overall situation, we must always refer the person concerned back to himself. Working in a group, with other people who go into resonance, facilitates this process considerably. Staying clear in such challenging situations needs a therapist who has worked and still works on their own inner victim and perpetrator-parts.

Establishing the facts

It is always helpful when the physical and psychological symptoms that plague someone can be ascribed to sexual trauma. The more the events of our sexual traumatisation can be brought out of their repressed and unconscious state, the more the split-off traumatised child parts feel seen and understood. It is not about reliving and retelling the sexual trauma in endless detail. It is enough to become emotionally aware of what has actually happened and to come into resonance and compassion with one's own child parts, which have up until now been kept in exile.

"When the memories come"

For a long time Sabine had resisted the truth of her sexual psychotrauma. As a result, she nearly ended up back in a psychiatric ward. Then she began to allow her memories to come, and actively tried to retrieve the images that went with them. This

Identity-Oriented Psychotrauma Thereapy (IoPT)

created intense feelings in her, and it was not easy for her to let these feelings come up without immediately fleeing into the refuge of her survival strategies: "Tonight there were so many waves of fear washing over me. Paralysing me. I feel sick, it makes me belch, like I'm going to throw up. I am frightened that I am not going to survive, that this time it [allowing the truth of the trauma to come up] will kill me. My teeth are chattering. It sits like a magnet on my heart and chest. I ground myself with both of my feet. I try to breathe deep into my abdomen."

So gradually the feelings of guilt and shame dissolve, because, as a victim, there is no reason to feel responsible and guilty, or to feel the shame; that actually belongs with the perpetrators and those who colluded with them. The child's need for love, closeness and physical contact are absolutely normal. Experiencing physical arousal, or even orgasm, during sexual trauma is not wrong either (Stoffers, 2018). It is the perpetrator who exploits the child's needs for contact and love, provoking the bodily reaction in the child and reinterpreting this reaction in his own way as desire. What the perpetrator did was wrong. He has every reason to feel guilty and ashamed. When the victim of a sexual trauma no longer takes up the victim position in the present moment, when he no longer feels ashamed or guilty, then self-denial and self-hatred can also stop. Then there is room for allowing our own pain and grief for what we have been through. Self-compassion can develop. Our own body can be experienced as something beautiful again, within which we can experience joy and sexual desire without fear, disgust or shame. Lust is then not a mere physical excitement and discharge, but the expression of a loving relationship with another person with whom we have a mutual sexual encounter. In this way, our own victimhood becomes part of our own history, it belongs to the past and no longer has to affect life in the here and now.

Back to the body

In order to feel good in our body, it is often necessary for us to work on the physical effects of sexual traumatisation, as the following example shows.

"I want to sense myself"

Henriette brought this intention. Over several years of IoPT-work she had realised the huge extent of her childhood trauma, including many years of sexual trauma by her uncle. He had repeatedly forced her with violence to perform oral sex on him. He had grabbed Henriette's head and squeezed her jaw so that she could no longer resist opening her mouth, and then he would stick his penis inside.

In this process of self-encounter with the Intention Method, her 'I' felt her lower jaw dropping open again and again every time she tried to close her mouth. TO SENSE went into resonance with this too, and helped Henriette to really feel this tension in her own jaw and to stay with it and not retreat inside herself. This made it clear why Henriette still has difficulty falling asleep at night. When she drifts off to sleep, her jaw muscles begin to relax and the lower jaw drops downwards. However, this body sensation runs contrary to the trauma survival mechanism still active in Henriette: "Fight back! Clench your teeth together and don't open your mouth!" When these connections became clearer to her, and Henriette felt that she had had no way of defending herself against the oral rape, her 'I' was able to relax, and Henriette felt more close to herself again. She found she could finally decide for herself to open and close her mouth without the unconscious fear of being raped.

In addition I learned something new from this piece of work about our 'want' in connection with trauma. Henriette's WANT was immediately ready to serve, it wanted to become active and *do* something. The person resonating with this WANT had little access to the subtle and very healing psychological processes that took place between MYSELF, TO SENSE and Henriette. Because the involuntary and unconscious processes in our body are not accessible to our consciousness, and we have had to banish the traumatic experiences from consciousness, we inevitably end up leaping into action, which although well-meant can do nothing to help overcome our traumatic splits. We often want to do something concrete, and do it straight away, even if it doesn't really help and doesn't change the split between psyche and body, but actually ends up deepening it.

Those who manage to regain access to their own physicality no longer feel the urge to cling to other people's bodies, seeking warmth, support and security there, and so be repeatedly embarrassed that this physical contact is sexualised by others.

Being me and constructive partnership

Anyone who works at exiting their psychotrauma biography, making sure to include their sexual trauma, has a good chance of a self-determined life and forming a constructive partnership with someone. I was very pleased to receive the following message from a woman who had been sexually traumatised during her childhood. Her partner had also worked intensively on his own trauma biography over the last few years.

"I say yes!"

"Your IoPT method has touched my life deeply and changed it in many ways. For the first time in my life I can say that I like myself and am happy! I remember asking you questions about my partnership several times over the last five years, since I first learned about your theory and method. The more I learn to take myself seriously, the more I realise what is acceptable to me and what is not in my relationship with X, whom I could imagine as my life partner. This year we celebrated the ninth anniversary of our being together. In the last five years of dealing with our traumas we have really grown together. Talking about our own traumas,

sharing our feelings and as best we can, seeing the other as having their own identity – I feel we are on the same wavelength now. As I learned to say 'yes' to myself, I also learned to say 'yes' to what is good for me. And so we can ultimately say YES to each other."

How to deal with perpetrators?

I suspect that many women, and men too, are reticent in seeking psychotherapeutic help, in no small part because they're frightened that a sexual psychotrauma could come to light. What if it turns out that my own father or grandfather was a sexual perpetrator? Who will believe me? How would I then behave towards my family?

Once it becomes clear that somebody has been sexually traumatised, many victims of sexual trauma ask themselves how they then should deal with the perpetrator, especially if he or she is still alive. Should I ...

- still keep in touch with them, because they are my own father or mother or sibling?
- deprive my own children of contact with their grandfather and grandmother?
- not tell anyone anything in the family not to turn the whole family against me?
- forgive the offender?
- maybe even talk to him and reconcile with him?

Here are some thoughts and experiences from the many self-encounters that I have therapeutically accompanied:

- Those who still feel they must have contact with the perpetrator probably still have internal child parts that continue to cling to the perpetrator, or their illusions of love about him or her. Those inner child parts do not yet feel love from the adult victim of the sexual trauma, and do not yet have any real trust in him or her.

- Anyone who turns their own children over to someone who has sexually traumatised them has not made much progress in processing their own trauma biography. They expose their own children to a high-risk situation in order not to admit – and therefore continue to deny – what the perpetrator actually did to them.
- If they consider the family with its obvious perpetrator-victim dynamic more important than themselves, they have not yet found their way back to their own identity. They are still needing the family relationships as a trauma survival strategy.
- Those who think they have to forgive the perpetrator are not yet with themselves, and still regard the perpetrator as more important than they are. They have not yet found the inner clarity to be able to live without the perpetrator, and cannot really be with themselves without reference to the perpetrator.
- This is even more true when someone thinks he or she has to, or even can, reconcile with the perpetrator. They are then still afraid of him and think they have to protect themselves from him, or they feel sorry for him and think they have to save him. These people are still stuck in their trauma of love.
- In general, in all these cases the person is missing their inner decisiveness and personal want, which means they feel that they cannot rely on their own life force, that they cannot protect themselves from the perpetrator, or that without the perpetrator they will not survive.

When such questions about how to deal with the perpetrator arise in a victim of sexual trauma, this is a sure sign that the trauma of identity and the trauma of love are still active, and that not all the parts of this person are yet aware of this reality. Further personal therapeutic work is necessary. According to my experience, this principle applies: involvement with the perpetrator, whether actual or even just in thought, causes further splits, and prevents the unification of the split psyche.

The psychological reference to the perpetrator or perpetrators makes a healthy identity impossible.

Someone who has processed his or her sexual trauma is, in the end, indifferent to the perpetrator. He wastes no more thoughts or emotions on him. He may not even call them 'father' or 'mother' anymore, because the perpetrator never had these fatherly or maternal qualities due to his or her own unprocessed traumas.

Therapeutic work with perpetrators

In general people come to me to work on their sexual victimisation. In their process, it can also come to light that this person, when they became a mother, because of their own sexual trauma biography, has not managed to prevent her own daughter from being sexually traumatised by her husband or father. Understandably, this evokes great feelings of shame in these women. However, these feelings can gradually be integrated in a healthy way as the mother feels her own victimhood more and more clearly. Her relationship with her daughter can then increasingly relax. Then it is no longer necessary to try to give her daughter the impression of being a good and loving mother – something that only came out of her guilty conscience. If the daughter is already grown up, then both life paths can finally separate from entanglement. The daughter gets a chance to take responsibility for her own life and shape her therapy processes in a self-determined way. The mother, in turn, can perhaps for the first time in her life do what she really wants to do.

Up until now, I have only been able to record a few experiences with men who have been sexual trauma perpetrators against children, adolescents or adults. It is clear that the term 'paedophile' is not helpful here, because usually they were sexually traumatised themselves as children, and so carry the accumulated pain of an entire trauma biography within them. They re-stage their own victimisation on children, often at the age when they themselves were physically, emotionally and sexually traumatised.

Probably the group setting, with which I prefer to work, is too challenging for sexual trauma perpetrators to make their perpetration public; but I am sure that they can only work through their perpetration, and let that go forever, if they have first acknowledged and experienced their own victimhood. At this point I can only encourage them to do that, in whatever therapeutic context. Even perpetrators of trauma know in their healthy parts what is right and wrong. Their healthy psyche wants to relieve itself of the feelings of guilt and shame. This is entirely possible in a private individual setting if a group feels too threatening.

My Personal Conclusion

Writing this book has helped me understand that our sexuality is an elemental force of our physical and psychological existence. As men and women we must take full responsibility for our sexuality every day and every moment of our lives. We must not delegate our choices about our sexuality to anyone else, not to a partner, not to our parents or friends, not to 'the family' or even to 'society', not to the pharmaceutical industry, not to the medical profession, not even to a therapist. It is necessary that we deal with our sexual desires, our lust, our love and the consequences in such a way that we do not split off from our body, our feelings and therefore from ourselves. Then we can agree with every decision we make and personally grow because of it. Until the end of our lives.

Much can be done preventatively in societies so that their members can develop a healthy human psyche, and develop their sexual identity in a good way. To do this, we must take our psyche seriously, learn more about it and protect it from early trauma. Instead of investing the time and the material resources available to us in trauma survival structures such as national, economic, military or gender competition, we could collectively do much more for our inner development. We could provide ourselves and all women and men who are parents and want to become parents, with sufficient time and material resources, so that they can prepare themselves and devote themselves lovingly to their children, especially in the sensitive first years of their children's lives. In 2018, total worldwide spending on the military was $1.8 trillion dollars and that figure is rising every year. Instead, imagine what could be financed in terms of meaningful material, educational and psycho- and trauma-therapeutic activities for the human family? We have the choice: to continue to struggle for survival or, together, do what is right and necessary for a good life for every woman, for every man and for every child.

Bibliography / Literature

Abendzeitung (6.1.2019). *„F***t eure Mütter!"- Sehr hohe Geldstrafe«* gegen Ribéry nach Mega-Ausraster. https://www.abendzeitung-muenchen.de/inhalt.bayern-star-rastet-auf-twitter-aus-franck-ribery-voellig-enthemmtgeldstrafe.5866f071-dca6-4d23-8d3a-50bcdc6510bb.html (accessed 14.3.2019).
Amendt, G. (1979). *Das Sexbuch*. Dortmund: Weltkreis Verlag.
Apothekenumschau (12.2.2019). Verhütung: Die Pille. https://www.apotheken-umschau.de/Verhuetung/Verhuetung-Die-Pille-52260.html (accessed 14.3.2019).
ARD (2012). *Die Story. Mama, hör auf damit!* Dokumentation. https://www.youtube.com/watch?v=Yr3_poVZBJE (accessed 14.3.2019).
Bange, D. (2007). *Sexueller Missbrauch an Jungen*. Die Mauer des Schweigens. Göttingen: Hogrefe Verlag.
Banzhaf, H. (2017). Trauma als Schlüssel zum Verständnis körperlichen Leidens. In F. Ruppert und H. Banzhaf (Eds.), *Mein Körper, mein Trauma, mein Ich*, pp. 104-142. München: Kösel-Verlag. (For English translation, see under **Ruppert** below).
Bauer, J. (2015). *Selbststeuerung. Die Wiederentdeckung des freien Willens*. München: Blessing Verlag.
Bauer, J. (2019). *Wie wir werden, wer wir sind. Die Entstehung des menschlichen Selbst durch Resonanz*. München: Karl Blessing Verlag.
Becker, L (2017). *Die »Pille« für den Mann ist da – nur wird sie keiner nehmen*. Bayerischer Rundfunk vom 09.02.2017. https://www.br.de/puls/themen/leben/kommentar-pille-fuer-den-mann-vasalgel-100.html (accessed 14.3.2019).
Biedermann, S. V. (2018). Sexuelle Funktionsstörungen nach Traumatisierung. In M. Büttner (Ed.), *Sexualität und Trauma*, pp. 95-115. Stuttgart: Schattauer Verlag.
Bischof, K. (2014). Sexocorporel-Sexualtherapie nach sexuellen Gewalterfahrungen. In M. Büttner (Ed.), *Sexualität und Trauma*, pp. 358–371. Stuttgart: Schattauer Verlag.
Bourquin, P. & **Cortéz**, C. (2016). *Der allein gebliebene Zwilling*. Köln: Innenwelt Verlag.
Boyle, T. C. (2019). *The Inner Circle, Bloomsbury, UK*. First published

Bibliography/Literature

Viking USA 2004; translated into German as *Dr. Sex*. München: Hanser Verlag.

Brochmann, N., & Støkken Dahl, E. (2018). *Viva la Vagina! Alles über das weibliche Geschlecht*. Frankfurt a. M.: S. Fischer Verlag.

Büttner, M. (Ed.). (2018). *Sexualität und Trauma. Grundlagen und Therapie traumaassoziierter sexueller Störungen*. Stuttgart: Schattauer Verlag.

Carnes, Patrick (New Ed. 2018) *Out of the Shadows: Understanding Sexual Addiction*, Hazelden Trade; 3rd edition.

Chamberlain, D. (1990) *Babies Remember Birth: And Other Extraordinary Scientific Discoveries About the Mind and Personality of Your Newborn*, Ballantine Books, USA. German edition: (2010). *Woran Babys sich erinnern. Über die Anfänge unseres Bewusstseins im Mutterleib*. München: Kösel-Verlag.

Coler, R. (2010). *Das Paradies ist weiblich. Eine Reise ins Matriarchat*. Berlin: Aufbau Verlag. [Ricardo Coler's book does not appear to be translated into English yet. It is available in many other languages such as French, Italian, German, Turkish and the original Spanish: *El reino de las mujeres*.

Dabhoiwala, F. (2014). *Lust und Freiheit. Die Geschichte der ersten sexuellen Revolution*. Stuttgart: Klett-Cotta Verlag.

D'Antonio, M. (2015) *Never Enough: Donald Trump and the Pursuit of Success*, St Martin's Press USA. Reissued as: D'Antonio, M, *The Truth About Trump* (2016), St. Martin's Griffin, USA.

de Waal, F. (2014). *The Bonobo and the Atheist: in Search of Humanism Among the Primates*, W. W. Norton & Company; Reprint edition (8 April 2014).

Duncker, H., & **Hirschelmann**, A. (2018). Der Rupturbegriff in der Psychopathologie und seine Folgen. In H. Duncker, R. Hampe und M. Wigger (Eds.), *Gestalten – Gesunden*, pp. 17-29. München: Verlag Karl Alber.

Emerson, W. (2017). *Geburtstrauma. Die Auswirkungen der modernen Geburtshilfe auf die Psyche des Menschen*. St. Nikolai: Moshammer; (2019) *Birth Trauma, the Psychological and Somatic Effects of Obstetrical Interventions*. San Francisco: Stonebrook Publishing House.

Evatt, C. (2017). *Männer sind vom Mars, Frauen von der Venus*. München: Piper Verlag.

Evertz, K., **Janus**, L., & **Linder**, R. (Eds.). (2014). *Lehrbuch der Pränatalen Psychologie*. Heidelberg: Mattes Verlag.

Finkenzeller, K. (2019). *Von wegen Superfrauen.* Publik Forum, 5, pp. 46–47.
Fischer, G., & **Riedesser**, P. (1998). *Lehrbuch der Psychotraumatologie.* München: Reinhardt Verlag.
Freud, S. (1972). *Drei Abhandlungen zur Sexualtheorie.* Frankfurt a. M.: Fischer Taschenbuch Verlag. (2011). *Three Essays on the Theory of Sexuality.* Reprint of 1949 ed. Martino Fine Books. [Also appears in *The Complete Psychological Works Of Sigmund Freud*, Vol 7: "A Case of Hysteria", "Three Essays on Sexuality" and Other Works. Vintage Classics. 2001 edition].
Freud, C. (2014). Mütter zwischen Karrierewünschen, Geldnöten und Zeit für ihre Kinder. In F. Ruppert *Frühes Trauma*, pp. 216–227. Stuttgart: Klett-Cotta Verlag. [For English ed. see below under **Ruppert**]
Fuchs, S. (2019). *Die Kindheit ist politisch!* Heidelberg: Mattes Verlag.
Garstick, E. (2013). *Junge Väter in seelischen Krisen.* Wege zur Stärkung der männlichen Identität. Stuttgart: Klett-Cotta Verlag.
Gray, John (1992) *Men are from Mars, Women are from Venus*, Harpercollins, USA.
Grossmann, K., & **Grossmann**, K. E. (2004). *Bindungen – das Gefüge psychischer Sicherheit.* Stuttgart: Klett-Cotta Verlag.
Grünberg, K. (2018). *Leichte Beute.* Publik Forum, 17, pp. 47–49.
Haarer, J. (1934). *Die deutsche Mutter und ihr erstes Kind*: München: Lehmanns. [An English discussion of the impact of Haarer's book can be found at: https://www.scientificamerican.com/article/harsh-nazi-parenting-guidelines-may-still-affect-german-children-of-today1/ (accessed 8.10.19)]
Häggström, S. (2016). *Shadow's law. The true story of a Swedish detective inspector fighting prostitution.* Bullet Point Publishing.
Harari, Y. N. (2017). *Homo Deus. A Brief History of Tomorrow*, London: Vintage. *Eine Geschichte von Morgen.* München: C. H. Beck Verlag.
Heiliger, A. (2000). *Täterstrategien und Prävention.* München: Verlag Frauenoffensive.
Homes, A. M. (2004). *Von der Mutter missbraucht. Frauen und die sexuelle Lust am Kind.* Norderstedt. [Not available in English]
Hoppe, G. (2014). Abtreibungen und Trauma. In F. Ruppert, *Frühes Trauma* (pp. 105–127). Stuttgart: Klett-Cotta Verlag.
Huber, M. (2003). *Trauma und Traumabehandlung.* Paderborn: Junfermann Verlag.

Bibliography/Literature

Huber, M. (2013). *Der Feind im Innern. Psychotherapie mit Täterintrojekten.* Paderborn: Junfermann Verlag.
Hüther, G. (2009). *Männer. Das schwache Geschlecht und sein Gehirn.* Göttingen: Vandenhoeck & Ruprecht.
Hüther, G. (2018). *Würde. Was uns stark macht – als Einzelne und als Gesellschaft.* München: Albrecht Knaus Verlag.
Hüter, M. (2018). *Kindheit 6.7. Ein Manifest.* Norderstedt: Books on Demand.
Javakhidze, N. (2018). *Die Beschneidung von Mädchen und Frauen.* Bachelorarbeit. München: Katholische Stiftungshochschule.
Kasten, H. (1999). *Pubertät und Adoleszenz. Wie Kinder heute erwachsen werden.* München: Ernst Reinhardt Verlag.
Kellogg, J. H. (1888). *Zitat im Wikipedia-Artikel John Harvey Kellogg.* https:// de.wikipedia.org/wiki/John_Harvey_Kellogg (accessed 31.12.2018). Here is the English equivalent; https://en.wikipedia.org/wiki/John_Harvey_Kellogg (accessed 8.10.19) [see the section on 'Masturbation Prevention']
Kerkeling, H. (2014). *Der Junge muss an die frische Luft. Meine Kindheit und ich.* München: Piper Verlag.
Kersten, E. (2017). Wer bin ich in meinem Körper und in meiner Sexualität als Frau? In F. Ruppert und H. Banzhaf (Eds.), *Mein Körper, mein Trauma, mein Ich*, pp. 300-313. München: Kösel-Verlag.
Kohn, A. (1989). *Mit vereinten Kräften. Warum Kooperation der Konkurrenz überlegen ist.* Weinheim: Beltz Verlag.
Koschorke, M. (2013). *Keine Angst vor Paaren! Wie Paarberatung und Paartherapie gelingen kann.* Stuttgart: Klett-Cotta Verlag.
Lee, B. X. (Hrsg.). (2018). *Wie gefährlich ist Trump? 27 Stellungnahmen aus Psychiatrie und Psychologie.* Gießen: Psychosozial Verlag. English edition: *The Dangerous Case of Donald Trump: 37 Psychiatrists and Mental Health Experts Assess a President – Updated and Expanded with New Essays* (2019). Thomas Dunne Books.
Lenzen-Schulte, M. (2015). *Leihmütter für Homosexuelle: Deine Zwillinge gehören mir.* faz.net vom 10.04.2015. https://www.faz.net/ aktuell/feuilleton/ debatten/leihmutterschaft-fuer-homosexuelle-13529689.html (accessed 14.3.2019).
Levine, P. A. (1998). *Trauma-Heilung: Das Erwachen des Tigers. Unsere Fähigkeit, traumatische Erfahrungen zu transformieren.* Essen: Synthesis Verlag. (1998) *Waking The Tiger – Healing Trauma.* USA: North Atlantic Books.

Bibliography/Literature

Loftus, E., & **Ketcham**, K. T*he Myth of Repressed Memory: False Memories and Allegations of Sexual Abuse* (1994). St Martin's Press, NY [Die therapierte Erinnerung. Bergisch Gladbach: Bastei Lübbe Verlag.]
Madeisky, U., **Parr**, D. & **Margotsdotter**, D. (2014). *Wo die freien Frauen wohnen.* Vom Matriachat der Mosuo. DVD.
Margotsdotter, D. (2016). *Am Herdfeuer. Aufzeichnungen einer Reise zu den matriarchalen Mosuo.* Rüsselsheim: Christel Göttert Verlag.
Maaz, H.-J. (2005). *Der Lilith-Komplex. Die dunklen Seiten der Mütterlichkeit.* München: dtv Verlag.
Maaz, H.-J. (2017). *Die neue Lustschule. Sexualität und Beziehungskultur.* München: dtv-Verlag.
Maaz, H.-J. (2018). *Die Liebesfalle. Spielregeln für eine neue Beziehungskultur.* München: dtv- Verlag.
Mausfeld, R. (2018). *Warum schweigen die Lämmer? Wie Elitendemokratie und Neoliberalismus unsere Gesellschaft und unsere Lebensgrundlagen zerstören.* Frankfurt a. M. : Westend Verlag.
Melzer, H. (2018). *Scharfstellung. Die neue sexuelle Revolution.* Stuttgart: Tropen Sachbuch.
Metz, L.A. (2017). *Der zerbrochene Engel.* Norderstedt: Books on Demand.
Miersch, M. (2002). *Das bizarre Sexualleben der Tiere.* Ein populäres Lexikon von Aal bis Zebra. München: Piper Verlag.
Mundlos, C. (2015). *Gewalt unter der Geburt. Der alltägliche Skandal.* Marburg: Tectum Verlag.
Nicon, L. (2011). *Befreit von alten Mustern. T.I.P.I. – eine Körperreise zum Ursprung unserer Emotionen und Ängste.* Paderborn: Junfermann Verlag.
Nick, S., **Schröder**, J. **Briken**, P. & **Richter-Appelt**, H. (2018). *Organisierte und rituelle Gewalt in Deutschland. Trauma & Gewalt,* 3, pp. 244–261.
Nunez, D. G. & **Schneeberger**, A. R. (2018). *Trauma unter dem Regenbogen: Stigmatisierung von Gender- und sexuellen Minderheiten.* In M. Büttner (ed.), Sexualität und Trauma, pp. 167–195. Stuttgart: Schattauer Verlag.
Orwell, G. (2002) *1984.* München: Heyne Verlag. Penguin Modern Classics edition (2004) (originally published 1949 by Secker & Warburg)
Palmer, B. (2018). *Wir können nicht allen helfen. Ein Grüner über*

Bibliography/Literature

Integration und die Grenzen der Belastbarkeit. München: Siedler Verlag.

Pease, A. & **Pease**, B. (2010). *Warum Männer nicht zuhören und Frauen schlecht einparken: Ganz natürliche Erklärungen für eigentlich unerklärliche Schwächen.* München: Ullstein Verlag. (2017 edition). *Why Men Don't Listen & Women Can't Read Maps: How to spot the differences in the way Men & women think.* 2001, UK: Orion.

Poiani, A. (2010). *Animal Homosexuality. A Biosocial Perspective.* New York: Cambridge University Press.

Precht, R. D. (2009). *Liebe. Ein unordentliches Gefühl.* München: Goldmann Verlag.

Preuss W. F. (2016). *Geschlechtsdysphorie, Transidentität und Transsexualität im Kindes- und Jugendalter*: Diagnostik, Psychotherapie und Indikationsstellungen für die hormonelle Behandlung. München: Ernst Reinhardt Verlag.

Rehder, U., & **Meilinger**, H.-G. (1997). *Sexueller Missbrauch – Straftat und inhaftierte Täter.* Krimpäd, 37, pp. 31–44.

Reed, D. (2019), *Leaving Neverland: Michael Jackson and Me*, HBO/Channel 4 (USA/UK) (UK based readers can watch the documentary at: https://www.channel4.com/programmes/leaving-neverland-michael-jackson-and-me/on-demand/63905-001 (accused 5.11.19)

Reich, W. (1971). *Die Massenpsychologie des Faschismus.* Köln: Kiepenheuer & Witsch. (1997) *The Mass Psychology of Fascism*, Souvenir Press.

Roddewig, M. (2012). *So geht Deutschland. »Flink wie Windhunde, zäh wie Leder, hart wie Kruppstahl«.* Artikel in dw.com. https://www.dw.com/de/flink-wie-windhunde-z%C3%A4h-wie-leder-hart-wiekruppstahl/a-16373027 (accessed 14.3.2019).

Rogers, C.R. (1992). *Entwicklung der Persönlichkeit. Psychotherapie aus der Sicht eines Therapeuten.* Stuttgart: Klett-Cotta Verlag.

Rogers, Carl. (1961). *On Becoming a Person: A Therapist's View of Psychotherapy.* London: Constable.

Ruppert, F. (2002). *Verwirrte Seelen. Der verborgene Sinn von Psychosen.* München: Kösel-Verlag. [Not available in English].

Ruppert, F. (2014). *Trauma, Fear & Love – How the Constellation of the Intention Supports Healthy Autonomy.* Steyning: Green Balloon Publishing. (2010). *Trauma, Angst und Liebe. Unterwegs zu gesunder Eigenständigkeit.* München: Kösel-Verlag.

Ruppert, F. (2016). *Early Trauma.* Steyning: Green Balloon Publishing.

Bibliography/Literature

Ruppert, F. (2019). *Who am I in a Traumatised & Traumatising Society?* Steyning: Green Balloon Publishing.
Ruppert, F., & **Banzhaf**, H. (Eds) (2018). *My Body, My Trauma, My I.* Steyning: Green Balloon Publishing.
Sulz, S. G., **Walter**, A., & **Sedlacek**, F. (Eds.) (2018). *Schadet die Kinderkrippe meinem Kind?* München: CIP Medien.
Sanyal, M.M. (2016). *Vergewaltigung.* Hamburg: Edition Nautilus.
Schwanitz, D. (2001). *Männer. Eine Spezies wird besichtigt.* Frankfurt a. M.: Eichborn Verlag.
Senf, B. (2004). *Der Tanz um den Gewinn. Von der Besinnungslosigkeit zur Besinnung der Ökonomie. Ein Aufklärungsbuch.* Lütjenburg: Verlag für Sozialökonomie.
Shaw, J. (2016). *The Memory Illusion: Remembering, Forgetting, and the Science of False Memory.* London: Random House.
Simkin, P., & **Klaus**, P. (2015). *Wenn missbrauchte Frauen Mutter werden. Die Folgen früher sexueller Gewalt und therapeutische Hilfen.* Stuttgart: Klett-Cotta Verlag. (2004) *When Survivors Give Birth: Understanding and Healing the Effects of Early Sexual Abuse on Childbearing Women.* USA: Classic Day Publishing.
Simon, H. (2014). *Nirgendland.* DVD. English title: *No Lullaby.*
Spiegel-Online (2.12.2013). *Epigenetik. Mäuse vererben schlechte Erinnerungen.* http://www.spiegel.de/wissenschaft/natur/epigenetik-maeuse-vererbenschlechte-erinnerungen-a-936692.html (accessed 12.8.2018).
SRF (11.02.2016). *«Sie wusste genau, welche Vergangenheit der Mann hatte».* https://www.srf.ch/news/schweiz/sie-wusste-genau-welche-vergangenheitder-mann-hatte (accessed 12.12.2018)
stern.de (26.7.2017). *Kindersegen dank Leihmutterschaft. So schaffte es dieses schwule Elternpaar, das vierte Kind zu bekommen.* https://www.stern.de/ tv/leihmutterschaft—so-schaffte-es-dieses-schwule-elternpaar-das-viertekind-zu-bekommen—7492800.html (accessed 12.8.2018).
Stoffers, A. (2018). *Das Lust-Dilemma bei sexueller Traumatisierung.* https:// www.zentrumensch-neuss.de/2018/11/05/das-lust-dilemma-bei-sexuellertraumatisierung/ (accessed 12.3.2019).
Stüvel, H (2008). *Zwitter – Mann und Frau zugleich.* Artikel in welt.de vom 20.06.2008. https://www.welt.de/gesundheit/article2126690/ Zwitter-Mannund-Frau-zugleich.html (accessed 12.3.2019).
Süddeutsche Zeitung (2.11.2018). *Wege aus der Finsternis,* p. 14.

Bibliography/Literature

Süddeutsche Zeitung (5./6.1.2019a). *Das Lachen des Vaters von Josef Wirnshofer*. Behind a Paywall at: https://projekte.sueddeutsche.de/artikel/gesellschaft/niklas-frank-e664522 https://www.sueddeutsche.de/muenchen/diakon-vergewaltigung-bewaehrungsstrafe-1.4311261 (accessed 27.3.2019).

Süddeutsche Zeitung (31.1.2019b). *Diakon erhält Bewährungsstrafe für Vergewaltigung einer 15-jährigen Messdienerin*.

Süddeutsche Zeitung (6.2.2019c). *So brach das Missbrauchssystem in Lügde zusammen*. https://www.sueddeutsche.de/panorama/luegde-campingplatzmissbrauch-1.4318817 (accessed 27.3.2019).

Tagesanzeiger (2.9.2018). *Die Geschichte vom armen Donny*. https://www. tagesanzeiger.ch/ausland/amerika/die-geschichte-vom-armen-donny/ story/11967238 (accessed 12.3.2019).

Tietz, A. (2017). Wechseljahre als Chance für einen Perspek-tivenwechsel. In F. Ruppert & H. Banzhaf (Eds.), *Mein Körper, mein Trauma, mein Ich*, pp. 335-348. München: Kösel-Verlag. English edition: (2018). *My Body, My Trauma, My I*, Steyning: Green Balloon Publishing,

Vasile, D. L. (2017). Gebärmutterhalskrebs und wie man eine Mutter wird. In F. Ruppert & H. Banzhaf (Eds.), *Mein Körper, mein Trauma, mein Ich*, pp. 314-319. München: Kösel-Verlag.

Von Weiler, J. (2014). *Im Netz. Tatort Internet. Kinder vor sexueller Gewalt schützen*. Freiburg: Herder Verlag.

WDR (2017). *Transgender-Kinder*. Dokumentation. https://www.youtube. com/watch?v=141CcfynjuM (accessed 12.3.2019).

WDR (2019). *Die Story. Wenn die Geburt zum Albtraum wird*. Dokumentation. https://www1.wdr.de/fernsehen/die-story/sendungen/wenn-die-geburtzum-albtraum-wird-100.html (accessed 12.3.2019).

Weber, F. (2018). *Welche Auswirkungen hat das Bindungsverhalten traumatisierter Mütter auf ihre Kinder? Was hilft betroffenen Müttern weiter?* Bachelorarbeit eingereicht an der Katholische Stiftungshochschule München.

Wickler, W. & **Seibt**, U. (1990). *Männlich – weiblich. Ein Naturgesetz und seine Folgen*. München: Piper Verlag.

Witteck, M. (2019). *Gewalt in der Geburtshilfe. Über traumatisierende Gewalt erfahrungen und die Relevanz einer selbstbestimmten Geburt*. Bachelorarbeit. München: Katholische Stiftungshochschule.

Bibliography/Literature

ZDF (2017). *Bordell Deutschland.* Dokumentation. https://www.zdf.de/dokumentation/zdfinfo-doku/bordell-deutschland-milliardengeschaeftprostitution-102.html (accessed 29.3.2018)

Notes

1. https://de.wikipedia.org/wiki/Geschlechtsorgan, (Retrieved 4.8.2018). The equivalent English page can be found at https://en.wikipedia.org/wiki/Sex_organ (accessed 8.8.2019)
2. To counterbalance this point of view see Gerald Hüther's book 'Männer – das schwache Geschlecht und sein Gehirn' (Men: the weaker sex and his brain) (2009) – not yet translated into English.
3. There's a lecture really worth listening to by Alfie Kohn on the subject of competition. It can be found at https://www.youtube.com/watch?v=S4si1HaDmLg (accessed 2.1.2019)
4. This is referred to as the 'Coolidge effect', which harks back to the American President Calvin Coolidge (1872-1933). The effect is named after a contemporary anecdote about the US President that runs like this: 'Coolidge and his wife Grace were visiting an experimental government farm and were being shown around seperately. She was amazed that there was only one rooster in the henhouse, and when she was told that the rooster performed the mating act up to twelve times a day, she said, "Tell that to my husband." When Coolidge himself was shown the rooster later on and told about it mating twelve times a day, he asked, "With the same hen?" - "No, Mr President, a different one every time." "Tell that to my wife," the President said.
5. 'Trans' from the Latin meaning 'beyond'.
6. 'Chrismon – Das Evangelische Magazin', October 2018 Issue, p. 41. (the original German magazine can be downloaded from their archive : https://chrismon.evangelisch.de/ausgabe/chrismon-oktober-2018-40734 (accessed 03/09/2019))
7. The film 'Female Pleasure' by Barbara Miller, which was released in cinemas in 2018, is very enlightening on this subject and worth seeing.
8. In the wake of the 1968 revolt, the attempted liberation from traditional sexual norms was, with hindsight, just another form of machismo under the guise of Enlightenment. The hero of the revolution earned the right to the most beautiful women. Something similar can be seen today with the Islamic State jihadists. They see women as their self-deserved spoils in the fight against the godless.
9. The Catholic Confessional Mirror for children (a guide to help someone examine their conscience in preparation for confession / the sacrament of

reconciliation) that was valid in my youth lists numerous behaviors in detail on the subject of 'Chastity' in relation to the 6th and 9th commandments. (Note: This is only a sin if something has happened voluntarily for unchaste pleasure. This has to be confessed.) Was I unchaste (shameless) in my thinking? Was I unchaste in speaking (shameless speaking)? Was I unchaste by looking at something? Or wishing for something? Have I behaved unchastely alone? Have I behaved unchastely with others? Have I allowed unchaste things done to me? Have I looked at bad magazines, pictures, films? Have I read bad books or passed them on to others?' http://k0104.kathhost.net/katechesen/bspiegki.htm retrieved on 12.8.2018
It seems that the Catholic Church has considerably lost its authority on the subject of sexuality in the meantime due to the numerous and publicly known cases of abuse within its own ranks worldwide. Therefore also the urge to sexually persecute others seems to soften and the above mentioned link is no longer to be found in the internet. Here is a more reduced version of a Confessional Mirror: https://www.erzdioezese-wien.at/dl/slMoJKJLMOMKJqx4lJK/Beichtspiegel_formatiert_farbig.pdf accessed on 28.12.2019).

Additional literature:
Ballmann, A. E. (2019). Seelenprügel. Was Kindern in Kitas wirklich passiert und war wir dagegen tun können. München: Kösel Verlag.

[10] 'Staufen im Breisgau' is the name of the town in Germany where this incident took place.. There is an English article documenting the case at https://www.tellerreport.com/life/what-mistakes-the-authorities-made-in-the-staufen-case-of-abuse.HJVQOLcHQ.html

[11] https://en.wikipedia.org/wiki/Erlkönig_(Goethe) (Retrieved 5.11.19) Translator's note: This poem by Goethe is one of the most famous pieces of literature written in German – every school child has to learn it. English translations however are variable in quality. The Sir Walter Scott version copied below is a very loose translation of the actual German and shies away from the sexual suggestiveness of the poem, as do most historic English versions. Literal translations however, lose the rhyme and rhythm of the original, so in the text we give a quite literal modern translation that has something of the scansion of the Goethe. Below is the Scott version.

Notes

O! Who rides by night thro' the woodland so wild?
It is the fond Father embracing his child;
And close the Boy nestles within his lov'd arm,
From the blast of the tempest to keep himself warm.

"O Father! see yonder, see yonder!" he says.
"My Boy, upon what dost thou fearfully gaze?"
"O! 'tis the ERL-KING with his staff and his shroud!"
"No, my Love! it is but a dark wreath of the cloud."

      [The Phantom Speaks]
"O! wilt thou go with me, thou loveliest Child!
By many gay sports shall thy hours be beguil'd;
My Mother keeps for thee many a fair toy,
And many a fine flow'r shall she pluck for my Boy."

"O Father! my Father! and did you not hear,
The ERL-KING whisper so close in my ear?"
"Be still, my lov'd Darling, my Child be at ease!
It was but the wild blast as it howl'd thro' the trees."

      [The Phantom]
"O wilt thou go with me, thou loveliest Boy!
My Daughter shall tend thee with care and with joy;
She shall bear thee so lightly thro' wet and thro' wild,
And hug thee, and kiss thee, and sing to my Child."

"O Father! my Father! and saw you not plain
The ERL-KING 's pale daughter glide past thro' the rain?"
"O no, my heart's treasure! I knew it full soon,
It was the Grey Willow that danc'd to the moon."

      [The Phantom]
"Come with me, come with me, no longer delay!
Or else, silly Child, I will drag thee away."
"O Father! O Father! now, now, keep your hold!
The ERL-KING has seiz'd me—his grasp is so cold!"

Sore trembled the Father; he spurr'd thro' the wild,
Clasping close to his bosom his shuddering Child;
He reaches his dwelling in doubt and in dread;
But, clasp'd to his bosom, the Infant was dead!

Green Balloon Publications

By Franz Ruppert:
Trauma, Bonding & Family Constellations: *Understanding and healing injuries of the soul* (2008)
Splits in the Soul: *Integrating traumatic experiences* (2011)
Symbiosis & Autonomy: *Symbiotic trauma and love beyond entanglement* (2012)
Trauma, Fear and Love: *How the Constellations of the Intention Supports Healthy Autonomy* (2014)
Early Trauma: *Pregnancy, Birth and First Years of Life* (2016)
My Body, My Trauma, My I: *Setting up Intentions, Exiting our Traumabiography* (2018)
Who Am I in a Traumatised and Traumatising Society? (2019)

By Vivian Broughton:
In the Presence of Many: *Reflections on Constellations emphasising the individual context* (2010)
The Heart of Things: *Understanding trauma – working with constellations* (2013)
becoming your true self: *a handbook for the journey from trauma to healthy autonomy* (2014)
Who Am I? Identity & Trauma, IOPT Theory & Practice
due out 2021

www.greenballoonbooks.co.uk
info@greenballoonbooks.co.uk

www.ingramcontent.com/pod-product-compliance
Lightning Source LLC
Chambersburg PA
CBHW030232170426
43201CB00006B/192